SHEILA NIELSEN

Job Quest
FOR LAWYERS

The Essential Guide to Finding
and Landing the Job You Want

AMERICAN BAR ASSOCIATION

Law Practice Management Section
Young Lawyers Division

Commitment to Quality: The Law Practice Management Section is committed to quality in our publications. Our authors are experienced practitioners in their fields. Prior to publication, the contents of all our books are rigorously reviewed by experts to ensure the highest quality product and presentation. Because we are committed to serving our readers' needs, we welcome your feedback on how we can improve future editions of this book.

Cover design by RIPE Creative, Inc.

Nothing contained in this book is to be considered as the rendering of legal advice for specific cases, and readers are responsible for obtaining such advice from their own legal counsel. This book and any forms and agreements herein are intended for educational and informational purposes only.

The products and services mentioned in this publication are under or may be under trademark or service mark protection. Product and service names and terms are used throughout only in an editorial fashion, to the benefit of the product manufacturer or service provider, with no intention of infringement. Use of a product or service name or term in this publication should not be regarded as affecting the validity of any trademark or service mark.

The Law Practice Management Section and the Young Lawyers Division of the American Bar Association offer educational programs for lawyers in practice. Books and other materials are published in furtherance of those programs. Authors and editors of publications may express their own legal interpretations and opinions, which are not necessarily those of the American Bar Association, the Young Lawyers Division, or the Law Practice Management Section unless adopted pursuant to the bylaws of the Association. The opinions expressed do not reflect in any way a position of the Section, Division, or the American Bar Association.

Printed in the United States of America.

14 13 12   5 4 3 2

Library of Congress Cataloging-in-Publication Data
Nielsen, Sheila.
   Job quest for lawyers : the essential guide to finding and landing the job you want / Sheila Nielsen.
      p. cm.
   ISBN 978-1-61632-963-1
   1. Law–Vocational guidance–United States. I. Title.
   KF297.N54 2011
   340.023'73–dc23

                                    2011018528

Discounts are available for books ordered in bulk. Special consideration is given to state bars, CLE programs, and other bar-related organizations. Inquire at Book Publishing, American Bar Association, 321 N. Clark Street, Chicago, Illinois 60654.

Contents

5   How to Start Your Quest   45

6   How to Get Knights and Wizards to Meet with You   59

7   What Happens in Meetings with Knights and Wizards   65

8   Friendship Lite   73

9   Interviews   81

About the Author

Sheila Nielsen is a leader in the field of career counseling for lawyers. She received her masters in social service from Bryn Mawr in 1973 and her J.D. from Temple University School of Law in 1977. After law school she worked as a criminal prosecutor, first as an assistant district attorney in Philadelphia, then as a state's attorney in Chicago, and then as an assistant U.S. Attorney in Chicago until 1984.

In 1983, Ms. Nielsen helped to create the Part-time Lawyers Network of the Chicago Bar Association and chaired that group from 1984-1987. In 1988, she helped to create a national association, Lawyers for Alternative Work Schedules, which she ran for two years.

In 1990, Ms. Nielsen developed her own career counseling and consulting service specializing in attorneys, Nielsen Career Consulting. For over twenty years she has counseled and coached lawyers with a wide variety of career issues including career path issues, job search issues, alternative work-time options, and career development. She provides guidance for attorneys with difficult workplace problems, such as dealing with a difficult boss, learning to delegate, managing time, and marketing. Many law firms utilize her assistance as an executive coach for partners and associates. She also assists many mid- to large-size law firms with their outplacement needs.

In 1994, Ms. Nielsen received an award from the Part-Time Lawyers Network of the Chicago Bar Association. In 2001, she was honored with an Outstanding Alumni Leadership Award from Lake Forest College. She has contributed to the field of career counseling and coaching by writing over eighty columns and articles appearing in the *CBA Record,*

Illinois Legal Times, New York Law Review, Legal Times of Washington D.C., Illinois State Bar Association Journal, Detroit Legal News, Florida Bar Journal, and many others. She has been an invited speaker over seventy times across the country at many conferences including ABA, NAWL, NALP, and Ms. JD, as well as many law schools and bar association meetings. She contributed to two ABA books for lawyers: *Breaking Traditions* and *Living with the Law*. She has done a number of MCLE webcasts and provides career advice on the LexisNexis website.

Ms. Nielsen is asked to speak nationwide on a variety of topics, including career direction, job search, marketing, leadership, career success, interviewing, time management, alternative work-time options, and many other topics.

Acknowledgments

This book was conceived over a bottomless cup of coffee and a stack of powdered sugar-dusted banana pancakes at The Original Pancake House, where my childhood friend, Mary Trimble, insisted that I had to birth this book some day.

When we were in junior high, Mary and I used to walk from our homes near the Northwestern University campus out to the large jumbled rocks piled along the edge of Lake Michigan. There we sat for hours, watching the waves, talking and wondering about what would happen in our lives. Mary was a gifted poet. She had to write. I was a dancer. I had to move.

Some forty years and many career incarnations later, we rediscovered our friendship. By then both of us had had three kids, been divorced, and rediscovered love with new guys. As predicted, Mary had become a writer. In my career I had evolved: from dancer to social worker to lawyer to career counselor. As predicted, I had to move.

Now in the middle of busy lives, we caught up when we could over pancake breakfasts. It was during one of these breakfasts that Mary insisted I write this book. She had been listening to me describe what I teach my clients about networking for a job, and encouraged me with her enthusiasm to get the message out to a wider audience.

Mary has been muse, cheerleader, videographer, editor, and therapist during this journey. She and her colleague, Michael Bai, produced a wonderful DVD that contains key concepts of the Job Quest. It can be found on my website. Thank you, Mary, for your pesky insistence. I am very grateful.

I also owe a huge thank you to my husband, Art, the love of my life, who is also my muse, cheerleader, editor, and therapist. His encouragement has been crucial through the many twists and turns of this trek to publication. Enthusiastic, passionate, determined, insightful, engaging and intelligent, he is a true helpmate and my best friend. His faith in this project has been essential.

Another shout out goes to our three kids, Jeni, Katy and Cindy. All of them sat through many years of many dinners, hearing me talk about and work out the concepts in this book. Apparently they were actually listening, as evidenced by their own various challenging and ultimately successful job quests. They have also been very supportive of their fourth sibling: this time-consuming literary progeny.

My father-in-law deserves a big thank-you. His knowledge of the business world, especially the way employers think about job creation and job seekers, has been invaluable. His steadfast encouragement and support have been immensely helpful.

My sister, Wendy, has also been a well-spring of sustenance. I could not have made it these past years without our many talks. She has helped my inner gyroscope back to center time and time again.

I thank my mother, a natural networker who taught me so much about being a true friend. She cared about everyone—taxi drivers, shop-keepers, neighbors, and strangers in need. Her friends and family had the benefit of her generous spirit. Unafraid to quietly think and act outside the box, she wore unique apparel when it pleased her, even when her children were appalled, and always remembered to watch the sun set in the vast sky, feel the wind, and really listen to the sound of the chimes. I wish she were alive to enjoy this book; it embodies many of the concepts she knew and used in her life.

I thank my father, who was both a brilliant electrical engineer and an accomplished pianist and teacher. He worked hard to be the best he could be at every endeavor, and was a model of perseverance. He was also my early role model as the unofficial career counselor for our extended family. Many of our relatives and quite a few of his piano students came to him for career advice. Dad and I talked about their decisions, and thought through ways to help them make the best choices for their lives.

Many thanks to the American Bar Association for making this book a reality, to Jill Eckert McCall who encouraged me to write it, and to Tim Johnson who has stuck by this project, and patiently kept the flame alive throughout this journey to publication.

Finally, I want to thank the many gifted networkers I have had the good fortune to counsel. They have taught me a great deal about what works and what doesn't work in a job search. I am indebted to them for their trust in me and for their many valuable insights.

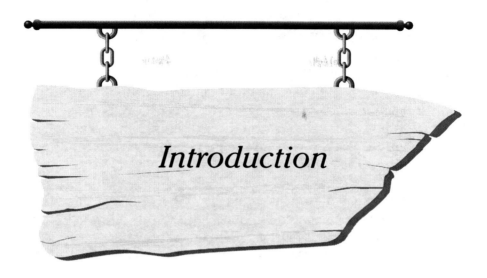

Introduction

Effective networking enhances job search luck.

The concepts in this book will teach you effective networking.

How do people find jobs? How do people *really* find jobs? Did you ever ask your friends that question? Chances are if you ask your friends, "How did you land your job?" you will hear this answer: "I got lucky. I was in the right place at the right time." When I first began my career counseling business for lawyers over twenty years ago, I decided to ask everyone I knew how they got their jobs so that I could learn how to help my future clients. Over and over I heard, "I got lucky."

This was not the answer I had been hoping to hear. I thought my friends' responses would help me understand the way people network effectively to land job opportunities. I had hoped to learn useful information for future clients, including those looking for jobs and having trouble finding them. What was I supposed to tell my clients, "Go out and get lucky"? That sounded like the worst advice imaginable.

However, after counseling and coaching more than two thousand clients over a period of twenty years, I have learned that luck and chance *do* play an important role in job searches. Some job seekers really are luckier than others. From my client's experiences searching for work, I've learned who gets luckier and why.

Lucky job seekers create opportunities for themselves, defying the odds when it comes to landing the jobs they want. By both coaching and learning from gifted job seekers in my practice, I have gained valuable information about how to have a productive networking search. I have studied the way these "lucky" people set their goals and then set about their mission to find work: engaging other people, enlisting their help, eliciting information, and overcoming barriers to success. I quickly realized that the way job seekers envision the process of networking and their attitudes about the process are vitally important for job search success. Lucky job seekers create their own good fortune.

Surprisingly, many of these natural networkers do not seem to realize how effective they are compared to typical job seekers. When questioned about how they landed their jobs, most are unaware of the strategies they used to create job opportunities. They give the standard response: "I got lucky. I was in the right place at the right time."

I have counseled many job seekers who did not understand or use particularly effective search strategies to create greater job opportunities. By contrast, these job seekers struggle to find opportunities, and many dread the process of searching for a job. And with good reason, since, for them, the process of job searching is a frustrating activity that does not always yield the best results.

For many people a job search is considered a necessary evil, a burden, or even a loathsome task that consists of writing the elusive perfect résumé, looking for ads, sending out cover letters and résumés, and hoping for the all important interview. All too often, people who approach the job search process passively, merely following the required steps indicated by the ad and waiting for the call back that likely never comes, experience a sense of hopelessness, resulting in few if any opportunities. After months of conducting their searches in this way, some of these job seekers drag themselves into my office looking and feeling defeated and frustrated.

"What can I do to land a job? What am I doing wrong?"

Most job seekers are motivated to put effort into their searches. Many simply need to devote their energies to activities that have a greater likelihood of developing job opportunities. In other words, they need to know what to do differently to create greater job search luck.

As my counseling practice evolved, I realized that I needed to share concepts and approaches I was learning from my lucky clients with clients who were not having good luck. I created a training session I called, "Job Search: the Quest." Once my clients had that training session, there was often an immediate difference in their attitudes and approaches to their searches. Learning this method was the fastest way to change job search fortune from bad to good.

I teach job search as a quest because the image of a mission with a goal—a quest—can have a positive effect on the attitude of a person with a difficult search. With these concepts and tools, you are in charge of your destiny. You are the hero of your quest. You take steps to rescue yourself by finding workplaces that fit your needs and that also need your help. You will succeed on this quest by facing your fears, and by using humor and creativity to meet with people who will help you to find your way to the workplaces that will welcome you. In addition, the iconography and imagery of the quest translates well to job search challenges, including understanding the overarching process of the search, identifying steps in the process, knowing how to think about your search and talk to your contact people in a productive way, as well as overcoming nervousness and fear.

The heroic quest is a universal image that people of all ages and backgrounds understand. From *Siddhartha* to *Star Wars*, from books about the medieval quest for the Holy Grail to videogames such as *Final Fantasy*, even the Olympic Games embody the quest motif. Many so-called left-brained lawyers, who begin with skepticism when I start our session on job search as a quest, tell me that this new conceptualization helps them to get their heads in the game in a way that nothing else ever has.

In my own life, I have had my share of difficult job search quests. After law school I was determined to become a prosecutor. I had gone to Temple Law School in Philadelphia, and I wanted to become a district attorney in Philadelphia. My friends, new graduates of Temple who had recently been hired by that office, told me that I needed a personal connection higher up than they were to have a chance to be interviewed. I had no relatives or friends that I knew of who could connect me to the D.A.'s office. But I found a way to get hired there.

After moving to Chicago from Philadelphia, I needed a part-time job while I studied for the bar exam. There seemed to be no way to find a part-time job as a lawyer. There were no ads in the local *Daily Law Bulletin* or part-time jobs listed in career resource centers at law schools. But after three days of looking for work, I was able to create a part-time position for myself with a matrimonial lawyer in town.

I was told that it was unlikely that anyone without a connection would land a job at the state's attorney's office in Cook County. I had no connection there, but I landed that job as well.

And finally, many well-meaning people told me that I was a long shot for a position as an assistant United States attorney, even though I was an assistant state's attorney with ample trial experience in state court at the time I applied for that position. There were hundreds of applicants for a few positions. I was not law review. I did not graduate from a top ten school. My two worst subjects in law school were criminal law and constitutional law. I had not worked as a law clerk for a federal judge. I was cautioned not to get my hopes up. People like me didn't get to be assistant U.S. attorneys. But I did.

For many years whenever people asked me how I got those jobs, I would tell them that I got lucky, and I believed that. But after years of working as a career counselor and watching and guiding hundreds of job seekers, as well as hearing hundreds of work histories from clients recounting how they had gotten their jobs, I realize that I had made a lot of that luck happen, just as the gifted networkers in my practice do. I was not very aware of what I was doing or how I was doing it at the time. I am more aware of the process of making good luck happen in retrospect.

That knowledge along with my own experience and the experiences of clients who get the job search training embodied in this book and conduct productive job searches as a result form the basis for this book. *Job Quest for Lawyers* contains the collective wisdom of many job seekers who found their way to good opportunities using the quest approach you will learn here.

1 The Hidden Job Market

To find jobs that are right for you, you must go on a journey into the hidden job market.

Your mission is to find the best possible jobs that fit your needs.

Your journey is a quest for a job.

A good job search is a journey from your current work situation to the job you want. When you start out you may not know for certain where you will finish, although you probably have some ideas about the kind of job you would like to find. But where will you gain the information you really need for job search success?

In the beginning of your job search, it is hard to tell where particular jobs can be found that will be possible options for you. That is because there is a unique and idiosyncratic mix of factors that affect your universe of options. What you will be able to attain is affected by such things as your core competencies or skills, your career goals, the current market, your personality, workplaces that are busy enough to hire, how you handle an interview, your motivation, and many other variables. There is no master list of workplaces that have jobs that are right for you. This is a frustrating situation. There is inadequate information for you to rely on as you begin your search.

Up-to-the-minute work world information is, by nature, elusive. Even if you could pin down exactly what is going on in the work place—

every current job held by every person, every company and firm that has work that you would be qualified to do—that picture would change daily because of shifts in work-flow, market changes (including global alterations), and decisions about who to entrust with business, not to mention changes in the status of workers including personal decisions about leaving or staying at a job. The marketplace of jobs and work that will match your unique needs is not easy to decipher. Since much of the market knowledge you need is essentially hidden from your view, it is challenging to try to figure out how to plan your journey to find the job you seek. When you begin your quest for a new job, it is as if you are behind a mountain and cannot see over the crest to identify the workplaces that could use your help and would welcome you. You cannot read a book about it. You cannot rely on Internet search engines to learn enough about it. Crucial information is concealed from your view, which is why you need to demystify it by conducting a quest.

In almost every other aspect of our lives we can read a book or look up a topic of interest on the Internet and learn what we need to know. But on-the-ground knowledge about where jobs exist that match a job seeker's particular needs is unwritten and constantly evolving. In fact, the work world is by nature a constantly shifting place where workplaces change quickly: a new branch of a large firm opens up; a group of lawyers leaves a large firm to open a boutique or join a smaller firm or move to a different large firm; companies decide to hire in-house counsel; other companies decide to use midsized firms for outside counsel instead of the large firms they used in the past; firms declare bankruptcy or merge with larger firms, sometimes without warning.

People—the workers themselves—also contribute to the instability of the work world. As goals and expectations for current employees change, personnel ebbs and flows. New parents take family leave. Some decide not to return for a period of time or at all. Junior partners move to different cities. People are fired. Senior partners retire. People harboring dissatisfaction about their current work situations make plans to move on. Worker status changes constantly.

The amount of work, or work-flow, also can be erratic, slowing to a trickle at times and then suddenly flooding the workplace. Employers are not always certain if or when they need to advertise or even start to look for more help. Employers may think it is best to hope that the current staff will be able to handle all the work. Then again, if more work comes along, will they be shorthanded, resulting in less than stellar job performance, which in turn might jeopardize future business? This sense of uncertainty is especially prevalent when the work world has been hard hit by economic upheaval.

In this era of reliance on Internet information it can be tempting to hope that the Internet will reveal the terrain that you cannot see. Unfortunately that is not the case. While the Internet provides valuable information, it will not reveal everything you need to know to have the most productive job search you could have. In part, this is because not all employers are using the Internet to find their hires. As a general rule, larger employers tend to post their jobs online. However, many jobs are never advertised. And even when the job is advertised, a large number of jobs, especially in midsize to smaller workplaces, are created because the work is there, the need for help has developed, and an enterprising and qualified job seeker with a positive buzz comes to the attention of the workplace through the grapevine.

For that reason job seekers have to rely, at least in part, on soft information—speculation, rumor, oral history, gossip, and hearsay—to learn where to find jobs that match their needs and skills. That is not your average lawyer's favorite way to gather information; it's closer to the way people communicated in medieval times. Although soft information is not always perfectly accurate, it can provide sufficient guidance to job seekers to point them in the right direction for their job searches.

To learn what is afoot in the marketplace for work, diligent and effective job searchers seek out informants or contacts who can provide valuable on-the-ground information. Done the right way, job seekers become knowledgeable about what is happening in the legal neighborhoods in which they may find work.

You *can* conduct a productive job search to find opportunities in the hidden marketplace. That search into the hidden job market is crucial to your job quest. To have a productive search you need to keep three key concepts in mind. These three key concepts consist of certain attitudes that lucky job seekers employ and two additional concepts that help to promote your search efforts.

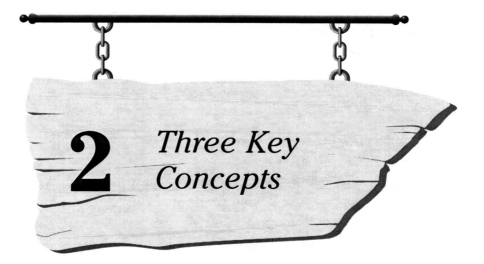

2 Three Key Concepts

For a networking job search to be productive there are three overarching concepts to keep in mind:

1. *Adopt Six Attitudes that Create Greater Job Search Luck*

2. *Spend Your Time Wisely*

3. *Knowledge Informs Luck—Be Knowledgeable*

Adopt Six Attitudes that Create Greater Job Search Luck

Traditionally, job seekers are told to network by talking to as many people as they can about their job search. It is true that job seekers have more productive searches if they are more interactive. But there is more that job seekers can and should do to have a productive job search. As I watch the luckier job seekers find their way to jobs they want, I have noticed that they either innately have or they adopt six attitudes that advance their search efforts. Highly effective job search-ers start with a sense of purpose and energy derived from a positive attitude. When they encounter problems, they work around them, and continue to advance toward their goals. They learn from their mistakes and push on in their mission. Many of these natural networkers also seem to know what to do next intuitively; they have a nose for job prospects and good people to connect with as well as what and how to say what they need to say to advance their searches when they meet with helpful people. They appear to have a well-spring of good sense

5

and boldness that helps them to figure out successful, sometimes creative strategies to advance their job search efforts.

Attitudes are not genetically predetermined gifts. Anyone can adopt attitudes that will help them to be more successful in their job searches.

Here are the six attitudes you should try to adopt and maintain during your search.

> *Be Interactive.* Be out and about and engage others in person as much as possible because your physical presence creates more chance opportunities. More magic happens in person.

> *Be Optimistic.* Cultivate and try to maintain a spirit of hope, good humor, curiosity and adventure as you engage in this journey that will get you to your goal.

> *Be Pragmatic.* Temper your optimism with realism. Be open to a change of course if you learn that you must gain additional skills or that you need to look for a less prestigious workplace just to gain traction or make somewhat less than you originally expected.

> *Be Intuitive.* As you search, be sensitive to and aware of the cues you obtain as you encounter helpful people and engage with them in your search. Trust your intuitive judgment.

> *Be Tenacious.* Motivation can wane in the face of challenges, but effective networkers find a way to buoy themselves by talking to themselves in a positive way as a supportive coach would do, and by enlisting the help of other people to encourage and sustain their perseverance.

> *Be Opportunistic.* Look for opportunities to advance your efforts. Use creativity, patience, inventiveness, and boldness to "work the point" like a tennis player or a basketball team, watching for chances, and "finding the hole" to advance your career goal.

Your attitudes matter a lot when it comes to creating job search luck.

Spend Your Time Wisely

Having the right attitudes is important, and it is also important to choose modalities for the search that will be likely to maximize a positive result. This is especially true when the economy is uncertain. When the economy is booming and jobs are plentiful, finding a job is easier. When the market is not producing a lot of jobs, even people with outstanding pedigrees can find it harder to locate any jobs at all, let alone land the jobs they want. Time can slip away and as time passes it may become harder to find work because the skills an employer is looking for are not being developed. Therefore, it is important to invest time in activities that are likely to yield results.

There are four standard search strategies that people use to find jobs: *ads, recruiters, mass mailings,* and *networking as usual.* The value of these approaches depends on the job seeker's particular circumstances. It is important for job seekers to assess the feasibility of spending time on each of these strategies and to consider whether the approach is likely to contribute to success.

An *ad* is like meat in a pool of hungry sharks. In the feeding frenzy it generates your resume can get lost in the brawl. Unless you are a clear match for the position being advertised you may be spending precious search time in an unproductive way. *Recruiters* work with a relatively small pool of lawyers. Their job is to fill an order for their clients, namely, the law firms or corporations that have hired them to do the search. Recruiters present only those applicants with stellar backgrounds who are perfect for the job orders they need to fill. Many lawyers do not get calls back from recruiters because they do not have the pedigree or skill set the recruiter must present. In addition, recruiters who present your resume to a potential employer are also trying to find your closest rivals to recommend to the same employer. *Mass mailings* or e-mailings are like cold calling with paper instead of using the telephone. It is an ineffective search method. *Networking as usual* consists of talking with everyone you know and telling them you are looking for a job. Unfortunately, when a job seeker talks about *needing a job* the result can be the counterproductive. People usually do not know of jobs to suggest to the job seeker, so they will often try to cut the conversation short and limit further interaction, telling the job seeker that if they learn of a job they will let him know about it. As a result the job seeker does not obtain important information that will help him find potential job opportunities that match his needs and core competencies. It can hurt your search if you use the "J" word too early.

Many of the "unlucky" people I work with are spending the bulk of their time in front of their computers answering ads and sending out résumés, hoping the recruiters will call back, and telling everyone they need a job. It is estimated about 70 percent of jobs are obtained by networking (Bureau of Labor Statistics). For most lawyers, even networking as usual is a better way to spend time compared to other approaches. But done the right way, the interpersonal networking method spelled out here is usually the best avenue for a productive search. Hard work in the job search context will be more likely to pay off and pay off faster when effort is directed toward well-informed, goal-oriented networking, geared to penetrating a job seeker's unique potential job market by employing key concepts and strategies that help the job seeker get luckier.

Knowledge Informs Luck—Be Knowledgeable

Attitudes matter, and spending time wisely matters, but something else matters almost as much when it comes to getting lucky in job searches. Louis Pasteur once said, "Fortune favors the prepared mind" (lecture at University of Lille, 1854). He was referring to the way that many scientific discoveries come to light. Some of the most important discoveries in science have been found by chance. Teflon was discovered that way, as was penicillin. Most recently, two scientists received the Nobel Prize for discovering graphene, a super strong, transparent conductive material made up of a single layer of carbon atoms that is remarkably strong and will revolutionize electronics in the near future. Graphene was discovered when these two scientists applied cellophane tape to a block of pencil lead and removed a thin layer of carbon. An untrained person could have and might have already created graphene by chance but never realized the valuable properties of the material captured on that tape. These two scientists had the knowledge to recognize the value of their discovery.

When it comes to luck in job searches, the same idea applies. For example, in the course of a search, you may already know the right people to ask for an endorsement, but you might not realize how important that personal endorsement could be for you. You may not know when to ask for an endorsement to increase the likelihood of the extension of an offer. If you recognize the value of that endorsement, and know who to ask, when to ask, and how to ask for that assistance, you are more likely to have good luck landing certain jobs. Recognizing the job search "graphene" when it's in front of you, so to speak, is analogous to the moment of recognition in a science laboratory. If you learn to recognize what you've already got going for you in your job search, you will achieve a better result. If you learn a new way to conceptualize your search and a vocabulary that translates your efforts into a meaningful construct that will guide you and keep you on track, you will get luckier. Knowledge informs luck.

The job quest approach provides that knowledge.

3 Blueprint for the Quest

A productive job search is a journey from your current situation to the job you want. Your attitude matters a great deal. Networking is the best way to proceed. But what should you envision to help you to have a productive search?

Think about your search as a medieval quest. You are the hero of this adventure. Your determination and tenacity, your energy and effort, your creativity, and even your sense of humor will make the difference in your ultimate success.

Let's begin.

Imagine yourself in your medieval *cottage* (your current situation/home/base of operations). Perhaps you need a new job because you have just been let go, or you want to move in-house or do government work, or maybe you are a new graduate. There you are in your cottage with your computer, working on your résumé, searching for and responding to postings online. If you have been looking for awhile, you are probably frustrated because you have been answering ads and getting very little result for your effort. You have probably sent your well-crafted résumé and cover letters to a lot of *castles* (workplaces) by now, but you have not gotten an interview, or you have been interviewed by phone and then dropped. You are getting worried and even a little depressed. What can you do to find a job if no one will even respond to your applications?

Frustrated, you leave the cottage to go outside for a break. In the distance beyond a clearing, you can see a forest and mountains, but you cannot see what lies beyond. How will you ever find a job when you cannot even see what's on the other side? The task of trying to figure out what is happening on the other side of the mountain seems overwhelming. You are tempted to go back inside, sit in front of your computer, and click on other castles' job postings. It may feel safer to answer ads all day long, but if you do that, you will encounter a serious and recurring problem.

Medieval castles are notoriously well defended, and these workplaces are no exception. They have moats, drawbridges, and a fire-breathing *dragon* (software scanners or other screening agents) stationed at the drawbridge to protect the castle from the advances of the horde of job seekers who are eager to have an interview. The *keeper of the castle keys* or *key keeper* (the person who has the final say about who will be hired) is the one person who has the true power to give you a job, but your résumé will not be presented directly to the key keeper if you send it through cyberspace.

The key keeper is hidden away in the castle to avoid detection by the mob of job seekers beyond the castle walls. When you send your résumé to the castle, it is delivered directly to the dragon. The dragon does not want to let you in. In fact, the dragon has strict instructions to find fault with your résumé and will try hard to find some reason to throw it in the moat or incinerate it in a blast of fiery breath. The key keeper is a very busy person, who has hired the dragon to ensure only the most qualified candidates make it into the inner sanctum of the castle for the in-person interview.

However, if you do your quest well, you may be able to avoid the dragon. And if you cannot avoid the dragon altogether, at least you will have people assisting you, your *knights and wizards* (helpful people), who will limit the dragon's ability to prevent you from entering the castle to meet the keeper of the keys and other castle staff. You will learn about these natural counselors and how to find and talk with them in Chapters 5 through 7. There are also castles that do not have dragons at the front drawbridge and may, in fact, welcome you into the castle. They tend to be the smaller to midsize workplaces.

As with most heroic quests, this one requires some bravery and some creativity. You will have to leave the safety of your cottage and venture into the forest where you will engage in an interactive and personal journey that involves talking with many people in a particular way to learn about the castles and villages, knights and wizards, and will help you to create trust relationships. Your quest for a job progresses as you move from trusted contact to trusted contact, learning more and more about the market and where you can locate castles that would be likely to welcome you.

You will also use the Internet and print media to compile a *master list* of people who are doing the work you want to do and workplaces that your research indicates could be likely prospects to target during your quest. We will discuss how to make this list in Chapter 4. You will grow and refine your list as your search moves forward.

In every heroic quest there are characters with whom the hero meets and interacts. Some are helpful and others are not. This quest is no different.

Although you will begin by talking with your own close circle of friends and colleagues, you will soon talk with people who are friends and colleagues of your initial group but who are complete strangers to you. That process of talking with strangers can be pretty daunting for many people. You do not know how they will respond to you until you try to communicate with them. You might risk being embarrassed or disappointed by them, especially if you have been let go or if you have been looking for work for a long time and you are nervous about how these strangers might react if they hear about that. You might feel you are uncertain about what to say because you have not done this sort of networking before. You will learn how to handle those situations in chapters 5 through 7.

Next, you will seek out people who are natural counselors who will meet with you and help you to find your way. These are your *knights* and *wizards* who are crucial for the success of your quest. Wizards are so well positioned and central to the castles and villages and so knowledgeable about the community you are trying to join that, if they are willing to help you, they can cut your search time significantly. It is important to know how to engage and talk with knights and wizards. Some of them will be so helpful to you that they will join your *round table*—your advisors, business associates, and personal friends who will help you during your quest and long after your job search is over. You will learn more about the knights and wizards of your round table in Chapter 5.

Much of your quest will take place in the forest. You are likely to feel that you are literally in the woods as you search for people who are natural counselors, find out about places that could work well for you, learn from helpful people about how to approach a particular castle, and learn about places that are busy, active, growing, and have a good reputation. You can meet knights in many settings. They might be at a conference you attend or you might learn about a knight from a wizard who was your professor, or you might consciously seek a particular knight or wizard out because you have heard this person will help you and is living in the village behind the castle and knows the castle staff.

One of the most effective ways to interact quickly with the community you seek is to join the American Bar Association and local bar associations and participate immediately in group activities. Get involved with the committees representing your target neighborhood and take an active role. For example, volunteer to organize the next panel discussion or conference or write a report for the committee. Your activity at the bar association will also enhance your ability to offer gifts of promotion and connection to the knights and wizards you will meet on your quest, which you will learn more about in Chapter 8.

As you go down the paths in the forest looking for helpful people who will tell you about the village or neighborhood you seek and the castles in that community, you will also encounter people who will not help you. These are *ogres*. It is important that you not lose heart if you encounter an ogre who discourages you or discredits you in some way. Part of the challenge of any quest is to stay undaunted in the face of difficulties that arise as you seek your goal. You will learn more about ogres and how to deal with them in Chapter 5.

The best way to advance your quest is to interact with the people in the forest and the villages. You must have brief *starter conversations* that you use to gauge whether the contact person you have met is a knight or an ogre. You will be able to tell this within the first few minutes of your conversation using the *voice test*, which you will learn more about in Chapter 5.

When you find knights or wizards in the forest, you want to try to meet with them in person for breakfast, lunch, dinner, or coffee because that is the best way for you to advance your quest. When you meet with each contact, you want to have a long, gossipy, rumor-filled conversation about what is happening in villages you are trying to join that may be known to this contact. You will learn about the castles you are interested in knowing more about. You want to hear about more knights and wizards who live in those villages or areas surrounding the castles. You will show your master list of people and places to the knights and wizards and ask them to help you meet more knights and wizards in the villages where you are trying to connect. You will tell the knights and wizards about your *goal and your challenge* or *dream and dilemma* and elicit their support to fulfill your mission by providing advice, information, and market knowledge, becoming your career counselor/market advisor. The content of your conversation with a natural counselor is discussed in Chapters 5 through 7.

Like the knights of the round table, you will also do *good deeds*. This quest is not just about you getting your job, it's also about helping and supporting those people who advance your quest and are nice enough to act as guides for you on your way through the forest to the castles you seek. You are creating trust relationships in the community you want to join and be a part of for the rest of your legal career. You are, in part, developing a team that supports and advises you in your job search, and you want to support and help them in return. This team is your own personal *knights of the round table*. You will read about the process of creating trust relationships in Chapter 8.

You will learn a lot from the knights and the wizards that you meet on your journey about finding the right castles, and you can also use your computer, another important tool for your quest, to learn about these workplaces and the people in them. Throughout your quest you will be looking for the castles that fit a *formula for landing jobs*, discussed in Chapter 4.

Throughout your quest, you will make choices about who to spend time with and whom you should pursue for in-person meetings. Although you want to try to meet in person with the knights and wizards who have the highest probability of helping you to have a successful quest, you never know who will turn out to be surprisingly helpful and have the information you need. You want to treat each of your contacts as a potential *treasure chest* and know how to get the box opened as discussed in Chapter 10.

As your journey evolves you will come to learn about other castles that could be a good fit for you based on your skill set and how it fits within that castle's needs and relationships. You want to use creativity and humor to find the people you are trying to connect with, and you always want to support and assist others who help you out. Creative networking is discussed in Chapter 11.

Through this search process you find places that might work for you that also have enough work to be motivated to hire. When that happens, you have reached the *tipping point* in your quest with respect to those particular castles as discussed in Chapter 12.

Once you know where you want a job and which workplaces would be likely to welcome you, at that tipping point, you shift into a *campaign to be hired* mode. You now want to look for the path that leads to the back of those castles. Behind every castle is a vibrant village full of people who know the castle staff and have the power to introduce you to them. A larger castle is far more accessible when you come in the side door or back door even if you must send your résumé to the front drawbridge where the dragon is stationed. You want to do your best to find a way to meet with the knights connected with the castles you have targeted in your quest. You use creativity, humor, and intuitive judgment to meet with people and you always help and support others in the process. Your goal is to go through a trusted contact to gain the attention of the keeper of the keys, staying mindful that you do not want to be a pest or overly aggressive in your efforts to do so.

Ask for assistance from people who know you, know your work, and trust you, and who, ideally, have some connection with the people on the inside of that castle. These are people who could vouch for you and provide you with *endorsements*. They can often help you meet with the keeper of the keys and other people connected with the castles. Sometimes you do not have those connections in the start of your search. Part of the challenge of the quest is to find these people, meet up with them, create trust and find out if they will support your campaign to be hired. Endorsements are discussed in Chapter 12.

If you conduct your quest the right way from the start of your adventure, you will meet people for breakfast, lunch, dinner and coffee, or in their offices, and talk with them. These meetings are called different things: informational interviews, informal meetings, formal interviews, or just lunch. Whether or not that meeting is called a job interview, it is a meeting that could lead to a job. You want to be fully ready for that meeting and comfortable with your message. Your message includes your reasons for leaving your current job, your dream and dilemma, articulating what you are seeking, how to teach your contact person to help you, and much more. The name of the meeting does not matter. What does matter is your readiness to have a good discussion. If you have a good discussion, you are essentially having an interview, and if you have a good interview, you are more likely to land a job. Interviews are the focus of Chapter 9.

In this Job Quest your overarching goal is to create trust relationships in the village or community where the castle is located and where you want to live for the rest of your legal career. The immediate goal of the quest is to find your way to meet with the keeper of the keys by getting an introduction from the knights and wizards connected to the castle. It is especially effective if you can come to the attention of the workplace through a trusted contact where the workplace has a need for someone with your background, there is work there that you are trained to do, and you have endorsements from people known to the castle staff. It is even more promising, but not essential, if you are the only job seeker knocking at the castle's back or side door. Even if the workplace has no current need, the castle may have a future need. Once you have created a positive connection there, your chances for being considered for a future job are enhanced.

This, in short, is the blueprint for a productive networking job search.

Many job seekers do not conduct searches that follow this method. If they engage in networking they follow a different approach.

Typically they try to talk with everyone they know and ask whether these people have heard of any jobs that could be good for them. But because they use an approach in which they start the conversation by talking about jobs right away, they often experience a disappointing result.

Most people you ask for advice do not know where the jobs are that would be good for you, and they will not be willing to take the role of being your recruiter. If you start out talking about where to find a job, if you use *the "J" word* too early, you run the risk that your networking conversations will be brief and uninformative. The contact person will usually say "I just don't know of any jobs but if I hear of one I'll call you." That is a very short conversation. You do not learn more information about the market or find more people to meet with or hear about specific workplaces or where the work-flow is increasing, or figure out how to reach the person in charge of hiring. You miss out on the gossip and rumors that can help to inform your efforts. It is important to understand why networking as usual is less effective and some of the possible pitfalls that can befall a job seeker. Job quest pitfalls are discussed in Chapter 13.

Done the right way, your quest will prove to be an invaluable help not only for your current job search, but also for your entire career. Searching for a job by creating trust relationships in the neighborhood where you want to live for your whole legal career allows you to create business friendships that sustain you throughout your career. These are the people who will be there for you if you ever need to find another job. These are the people who provide the basis for future business development. In the world we live in where job security is swiftly becoming a thing of the past, we all need strong networks to keep our careers afloat.

Success in your quest will depend on such things as your ability to learn where the work is, figure out where you fit into the market, be your own recruiter, be creative about how to meet with the knights and the wizards, be assertive but not aggressive, be bold but not obnoxious, be persistent but not a pest, learn about the castles and surrounding villages, learn how to talk with the knights and wizards, help them do a better job of helping you to advance your search, create a positive buzz about yourself in the neighborhood where you want to work, and use humor and have fun in the process, as well as many other key concepts we will talk about in this book.

There are also some activities that will help you to get ready for the quest. They will help your quest to be more focused and proceed more quickly. You can read about them in the next chapter.

Let's start.

Checklist and Guide for Your Job Quest

1. Do you want the same type of job? Do you want to find a job in the same practice area?

    If not, do exercises that help you find your career "sweet spot":

    ❏ AILS:

    > *Aptitude, Interest, Lifestyle, Self-Actualization*

    ❏ ESSENTIAL ELEMENTS

    If you want the same type of job, you may skip over the "sweet spot" exercises and go directly to QUEST PREPARATION CHECK-LIST.

2. QUEST PREPARATION CHECKLIST:

    ❏ Create a **basket of skills** resume

    ❏ Locate the **work-flow**

    ❏ Create a **master list of people and places**

    ❏ Know the **formula for landing jobs**

    ❏ Articulate your **dream and dilemma**

    ❏ Create a To Do list

    If you are feeling upset or depressed:

    > ❏ Do a **mental status check** before you set out
    >
    > ❏ Get support or help if you need it

    ❏ Be prepared for your interview before you set out

3. GUIDING PRINCIPLES FOR THE QUEST:

    ❏ Start your quest with close friends (knights/wizards)

    ❏ Meet with people suggested by your knights/wizards

    ❏ Try to meet more villagers in the right neighborhood by going to conferences, meetings, and other places frequented by that group

    ❏ Do your networking in person as much as possible

    > *Breakfast, lunch, dinner, or coffee*

❐ Expand your encounters with knights/wizards everywhere
you go

Use the **starter conversation**

Avoid the "J" word when you start out

Try to have long, gossipy, rumor-filled conversations to learn more

Use the **voice test**

The voice of the natural counselor goes up

Be open and engaging, creative and bold

But not aggressive or a pest

Cultivate lucky attitudes:

Interaction

Optimism

Pragmatism

Intuition

Tenacity

Opportunism

Consult the knights and wizards of your roundtable when you
question your judgment or need help

❐ Look for **treasure chest** people

You never know. . . .

❐ Use **creative networking** to enhance your luck

Being careful to conform to workplace practices

4. GUIDING PRINCIPLES FOR IN-PERSON MEETINGS

In conversations with knights and wizards follow these principles:

❐ Create a **zone of comfort** first

Friendship lite

Trust relationships

❐ Discuss your contact's **biography**

. . . but do not get stuck on that topic

❐ Tell your knights/wizards your **dream and dilemma**

Describe your goal

Explain your problem

❏ Focus the conversation on your **master list**
  People doing the work you want to be doing
  Places or castles you seek

❏ Learn the on-the-ground information:
  Gossip (what is happening in the village)
  Work-flow (busy, active, growing work places)
  Culture of the place (people like to work there)
  Try to learn the keeper of the keys

❏ Give your knights/wizards clear **prototypes**
  Illustrations of castles you are seeking

❏ Find more **nice people** in the village to learn from
  Everyone knows who is nice and who is not

5. DO GOOD DEEDS

❏ Give back to your knights and wizards
  Create a positive buzz
  What goes around comes around

❏ Gifts or good deeds
  Listening
  Information
  Connection
  Promotion
  Tangible gifts such as books or CDs if appropriate

6. ONCE YOU KNOW A LIKELY CASTLE, YOU REACH
A TIPPING POINT: MOVE FROM QUEST TO CAMPAIGN
WITH RESPECT TO THAT CASTLE

In your campaign to be hired follow these principles:

❏ Use the formula for landing jobs
  Your skill set matches the needs of the workplace
  The work-flow is there
  You try to come to their attention via a trusted contact
  Your background matches well

☐ Ask for endorsement if the elements are there

Your contact knows you, likes you, knows your work

Your contact knows someone on the castle staff who is respected or a gatekeeper

There could be a need for help at this castle

☐ Seek out villagers and others who could help you find the keeper of the keys or meet other staff

Keep developing trust relationships

7. REACH THE GOALS OF YOUR JOB QUEST:

☐ Find and meet the key keepers and have an excellent interview every time

☐ Create a supportive network of knights and wizards who will help and sustain you for your entire career

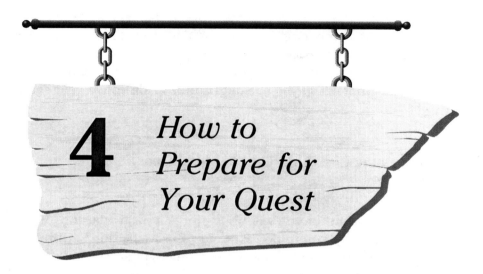

4 How to Prepare for Your Quest

There are eight steps that will help you be prepared for the time when you are in the forest trying to find knights and wizards. You want to be ready for those conversations. It is important to do the eight step preparation because it will provide you with important information and knowledge about yourself to help you to help others guide you in your search for the right job.

Step One: Figure Out Your Career Sweet Spot
- The AILS Test
- The Essential Elements for Your Career

Step Two: Create a Basket of Skills Résumé

Step Three: Locate the Work-flow in Your Legal Neighborhood

Step Four: Create a Master List of People and Places You Want to Explore

Step Five: Learn the Formula for Landing Jobs

Step Six: Articulate Your Dream and Dilemma

Step Seven: Create a To Do List

Step Eight: Do a Mental Status Check

Would you go on a trip to Europe, Africa, or Japan without packing your bag? Would you go hiking without boots and a map or GPS system to guide you? Would you set off on a sailboat without knowing how to work the sails? Preparation for a journey can make all the difference in the success of the venture. You are the hero of this quest, and it is up to you to conquer challenges and find your way to the castles that will fulfill your mission. It is important to perform this eight-step preparation, because it will provide you with important information and knowledge about yourself so you can help others guide you in your search for the right job.

Step One: Figure Out Your Career Sweet Spot

The AILS Test

How do you know whether you will be happy in a particular job? What four elements can help you to predict your job satisfaction? *A*ptitude, *I*nterest, *L*ifestyle, *S*elf-actualization. These elements create the acronym *AILS*. They can help you figure out *what AILS you.* If you have these four elements in your job, it is highly likely that you will enjoy your career and be relatively happy going to work. If your current job is not satisfying, or if sometime in the future you feel dissatisfied with your job or career, this exercise will help identify the source of your dissatisfaction.

Aptitude. How well do you understand the work you need to do for the job? If the work is easy for you, generally speaking, and you understand what you need to learn and learn it quickly, you probably have an aptitude for this work. How do you know if you have an aptitude? Where others might struggle for comprehension, you already get it, or learn it quickly. When you studied this subject in school, you did well with reasonable effort. Colleagues, professors, or supervisors tell you that you are a quick study. If you do not know what your aptitudes are, there are testing services that can help you identify them.

Interests. Interests and aptitudes are not the same. You can be very interested in a subject but lack the aptitude. You can have an aptitude but lack interest in the subject.

Many lawyers who do not enjoy the practice of law report a lack of interest in legal or law-related subject matter. Given a wide array of books or magazines to read, they would not choose to read about matters related to the law. If you lack interest in the work you do, the content of your daily work is likely to be boring for you. Ultimately that lack of interest makes it hard to continue to do an outstanding job. If you do not like thinking about legal issues and you are a lawyer, that is a serious career issue.

Another issue that arises around the concept of interest has to do with a strong interest or passion for a career or job that is not reasonably achievable. For example, you would love to be a film critic or write the next great thriller series, but you are a lawyer, you have a young family, and you want to keep making six figures. You should try to build in elements of the kind of work you love as a hobby or do some of what you love during your leisure time. You might be able to write a blog or write a column for a legal magazine. If you have other unmet strong interests in helping others, you might try to engage in community service, volunteer work, or other activities that satisfy that need to some extent. Eventually, you may be able to transition your career in a direction that includes more of your passions or strong interests depending on what they are and your particular situation. You may want to complete Exercise 2 in Appendix A, "Find Your Career Sweet Spot."

Lifestyle. What kind of lifestyle do you need to be satisfied? Maybe your highest priority is to have a balance between your work and your home life. Maybe you need to be sure you can leave your stresses and worries at work and not take them home with you. Perhaps you believe you need to make six figures to feel secure. Perhaps you need to make enough money to support a growing family and allow your spouse to be home with the children. These and other elements influence your lifestyle satisfaction level. Exercise 3 in Appendix A will help you identify what you need to have to achieve the lifestyle you envision for yourself.

Self-Actualization. What kind of person do you want to be? The culture of your workplace has an impact on you. How you respond to the people you interact with at work, your clients, the work you do, the pace of your work, and your colleagues' attitudes all interact with your unique personality to shape the person you are and are becoming. If you work in a pressure-cooker environment that makes you feel irritable and you bring that attitude home with you, creating tension in your family, your workplace environment may be having a negative impact on your life outside of work. Your behavior is being shaped in a way that is likely to create a negative response in people around you both outside of work and in the workplace. You might attempt to combat it by trying to ignore what is happening at work. But it is not easy for most people to change their natural responses to their work environments. The same intense workplace culture that makes you crazy could be a great environment for someone who thrives on being in a hectic or fast-paced setting. That person might enjoy the beehive-of-activity aspect of the workplace and not experience it as overly stressful. Every person's path to self-actualization is unique.

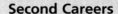

Second Careers

Many lawyers find a way to develop a second career over time while relying on their legal careers to fund that venture. Some lawyers create second careers by gaining credentials in new fields, while others create businesses. For example, a lawyer with a passion for designing wedding dresses continued to work as a lawyer, while her sister created a wedding gown business in New York. It was gratifying for her to be able to fund the business and be involved in its evolution. She may eventually transition her career to work there full time and leave the law altogether. Another lawyer, a partner at a midsize firm, developed a series of weight loss clinics while he continued to work as a lawyer. He built up the business for a number of years, eventually leaving the law once the clinics were doing well enough to provide him with a good income. Another lawyer transitioned to a career in interior decorating by helping her husband's business furnish and decorate corporate offices. That experience allowed her to move into a new field without the re-credentialing needed for some other fields. Other lawyers have created second careers becoming psychologists, teachers, writers, journalists, restaurateurs, and much more. Unless friends and family open the door to a radically new career, many lawyers may need to re-credential. An exception to that general rule can sometimes occur if the new career is one that serves the legal field or makes use of knowledge of the law even though the person no longer functions as a lawyer, per se. Examples of these careers include legal recruiter, director of career services for a law school, marketer for a law firm, legal publisher, journalist for a legal magazine, director of legislative affairs for a company, trust officer at a bank, compliance positions, dean of students, and financial planner. Careers related to the legal field can serve as a training ground for a totally new career direction, allowing the lawyer to skip over formal education that would normally be required to qualify for the new career.

How is the workplace culture affecting you? Do you like the person you are and are becoming? Or do you go through your day feeling drained, bored, angry, annoyed, or anxious? Are you bringing your stresses home with you? Are you spending so much time by yourself in front of your computer doing research that you are feeling disconnected and depressed? Do you need a more social, team-oriented workplace? If you are required to work fast under pressure, are you finding that to be a challenge that adds to your sharpness or are you feeling overwhelmed? If you have to be decisive to excel on the job, is that making you tougher or are you becoming bitter? Does the work you do or your workplace culture require that you compromise your ethics or honesty?

The work we choose to do and the place we choose to work have the power to shape our personalities. You want to be sure you like the result you are getting. If you don't, you may need to find a different environment or, in some cases, a different career. What works well for one person does not always work well for another, so solutions vary: changing partners or practice groups, moving to a new law firm, going in-house, or into government might do the trick. Sometimes more radical steps need to be taken, such as changing your career altogether. You may want to complete Exercise 4 in Appendix A at this point to determine your level of self-actualization.

Finding a Better Fit

A number of years ago I worked with an energetic, hard-working associate who began her career in labor and employment law with a socially engaging, sensitive personality. After years of courtroom battles, however, she had become a tough-minded, abrasive litigator, which helped her to succeed in her job but caused problems in her life. She brought that attacking attitude home with her, and not only had sleepless nights and headaches, but also fought with her first husband over "every little thing." They divorced. About a year later, she met a wonderful man and they decided to get married. She came to me for career counseling because she was worried that she would ruin her second marriage if she continued to practice law as a litigator. Being a litigator brought out her ferocious inner warrior, but she did not like the effect on her personality or the toll on her health. After considering alternatives, she decided to move into the field of human resources as an HR coordinator for a midsize company and was able to make that transition doing an effective networking search. This transition permitted her to soften her personality and relax into the role of a more collegial team member. She was even more successful in this career than she had been as a litigator because the setting allowed her to utilize many of her personal strengths, and natural sociability.

The Essential Elements for Your Career

Knowledge Informs Luck—Be Knowledgeable. What do you need to be successful in your work life? For a job to be satisfying on a long-term basis you want to be sure the workplace satisfies your personal needs. If you are unhappy with your job, you are more likely to leave or be fired. This is not good for your career or your self-esteem. You want to have a job that plays to your strengths as a person as well as contributes to your professional skills. If you know what you are looking for, you can vet the workplace for your needs.

The Essential Elements exercise helps you to identify those elements you need in your career and your work life to be satisfied and those irritants to avoid because you are allergic to them. This exercise is very useful to help you figure out what you need in a job, and to identify the sweet spot for your career. It helps you to create your unique template for a satisfying work life and find the matches for that in the field of potential workplaces. Start with a work history, as illustrated in Appendix A on page 153. The importance of the work history for purposes of this exercise is the plus/minus columns, not the work history itself. Identifying what you liked and disliked about each job is the key to spotting trends that will affect your choice of future workplaces.

To do your work history, write down every job you have had, paid or unpaid, including volunteer work. Then create a plus and a minus column for each job and list everything you liked or disliked about each position. Include college and law school as well. When you have finished this list, look at it carefully and try to discern key trends. You can ask friends and family to help you with this endeavor if you need assistance to spot the trends. A trend might be that you always seem to like a job if you like the people with whom you are working. Or you usually hate jobs when you have to work under stress or feel bored. Everyone has a unique profile that emerges from this exercise, but the trends often stand out if you look for them. These trends usually reveal consistent and powerful needs that you have to meet to have a satisfying work life. From these trends you can create two lists: one is a list of your "Essential Elements" and the other is your "Irritants to Avoid."

Do the work history, spot the trends, and then write them down. The trends become your Essential Elements. These elements are the ones you want to have in your work life to be satisfied. Do you need to have the role of the problem-solver or the expert or the advisor? Write down the roles you want to have as part of your work life on your list of Essential Elements. Do you require an uptick on the learning curve to stay engaged? Put *mental variety* on the list. Do you need stability and security? Put *stability/security* on the list.

Next, create a second list of all the elements you can find from your work history that make you annoyed, irritated, angry, or feel some other negative experience that you would like to avoid. Does a micromanaging boss or lack of control over your hours make you very upset? What pushes your buttons? Try to list only those irritants that make you feel truly allergic. These go on your Irritants to Avoid page.

After you have your two lists, create a scale next to each element. The scale should range from 1 to 10. Appendix A, page 159, has an illustration. Next, give every element you have identified a grade on a scale of 1 to 10, with 10 the most positive rating. Each element gets a separate rating. You are rating how much you want to have this element in your work life. If you give something on your list a 9 or 10, that means you really should not take a job if it does not provide that element. If you give an element only a 4 or lower, you should consider taking it off of your list because it is not essential enough to make a difference in your choice of a particular job.

When it comes to grading the list of elements you want to avoid, you are measuring how much you hate that element. If you give something a 10, you would not want to take a job that would require that you put up with that element in your daily work life. For example, if you do not work well under pressure and you hate pressure so much you give it a rating of 10, then you should try to avoid jobs that require that you deal with intense pressure on a daily basis. If, however, you dislike pressure but you give it a 6, that would indicate that you could manage some pressure even if you do not like it. You would look for jobs where you only have to cope with moderate pressure on a daily basis.

Once you have two lists of elements reflecting what you need to have and to avoid in your work life and you have graded each element, you have a template of your work life requirements. You can use this template to measure or vet a potential job for your unique needs. As you learn more about a workplace over the course of your quest, you will be able to make fairly accurate guesses about how well that particular workplace is likely to match your needs. The template also helps guide you during your quest in asking questions that will give you the information you need to assess whether the job you are considering will be a good match for you. For example, if a micromanaging boss is on your list of irritants, you want to discreetly ask questions as you network with people loosely affiliated with a given workplace to learn how the workplace is managed. Discovering a micromanager should be a factor in your decision to work there or to keep looking for a workplace that might be a better fit for you.

The template you create can change over time, so it is a good idea to update your template over the course of your career. A change in priorities can occur in your life that will affect the essential elements or irritants you feel most strongly. For example, if you have a baby and feel strongly that you want to have predictable time to be with your child, the need for a balance between work and home life might suddenly pop to a 10 on your Essential Elements list. The irritant of being unable to control your hours might jump to a 10. This change in priority may affect your job satisfaction and your need to make a career change.

Once you create your template, you can apply it to your current job to learn what is satisfying and not satisfying for you when it comes to your present work life. You are essentially vetting your workplace for your needs. For example, if you currently have a job that does not allow you a chance to have variety and you assign a 9 to that element but you are getting a 2 from the current job, then the job is flunking when it comes to that important need. You can get along for a while with a serious mismatch such as that, but over time it will take its toll. If you are missing out on many of your deeply felt needs, you may want to launch a job quest to find a job that is a better fit for you.

Step Two: Create a Basket of Skills Résumé

If you are an employer looking for someone to help you, you want to find a likeable person who also has the core competencies needed to do the job well. As a job seeker, you have to understand the skills and background you possess so that you can show the employer you have what it takes to do the job needed. Your résumé is your chance to tell the prospective employer your unique story. It is an advocacy piece. Your résumé is also a marketing piece that could convince the employer to meet with you for the all-important interview, whether it's formal or informal.

To create a good marketing piece, be sure your résumé conveys the following basic information to the prospective employer:

> The kind of job you want to have
> Your qualifications for that job
> Where you worked and who you worked for in the past
> Illustrations of success, especially doing comparable work

There are a number of excellent books on the topic of résumé writing, some of which are listed on the ABA's website site at www.lawpractice.org.

There are a variety of résumé formats that you could use to convey your information. Most lawyers choose a chronological résumé style. That format shows relevant education, employment history, and experiences listed in chronological order starting with the most recent experience. The chronological résumé format highlights a consistent work history. If you have been working at one place for your entire career and you want to showcase your loyalty or show that you have worked your way up the ladder at one workplace, the chronological format can do that.

The chronological résumé may present some problems when it comes to networking, however. It lists each job followed by a description of the work you did there. Often, the same or similar skill set is described again and again under each job listed. The problem is that in a networking meeting, over lunch or coffee, the person reviewing your résumé will only have a moment to glance at it. You want the focus of the meeting to be your talk together. With a chronological résumé, the reader has to dig out the relevant skill set written under each job heading. A résumé can be cleaner and clearer if skills are listed just once at the top of the résumé. That "basket of skills" or skills-based format can provide an immediate, clear understanding of skills that you want the reader to see. You want your contact to think, "I like this person and—how lucky!—she has the skill set I am looking for." Or, "I bet my friend (an overworked partner at a litigation boutique) could really use this person's help."

You can also choose to include or exclude the core competencies you want to emphasize or de-emphasize based on the type of job you expect to learn about in your networking meeting. For example, if you have been working as an environmental lawyer on the litigation side, but you will be talking with an in-house counsel about compliance work at her corporation in your informational meeting, you can highlight the skills you possess that are useful for compliance work at the top of your résumé. If your résumé highlights litigation skills, the person you are meeting with might not think you would be a good addition to her department, when you really could be a good match. Appendix B includes examples of this basket of skills résumé.

Step Three: Locate the Work-flow in Your Legal Neighborhood

The success of your search may depend to a great degree on how well you identify where the work is more abundant as it relates to your skills. You want to look for jobs where you have a greater likelihood of being hired because your assistance is needed. When employers have a good flow of work, they are thinking about if and when to hire new people to join the team or to replace those who have left. That's when you show up. Or, you may have already shown up, and the people at that workplace remember you because they met you and liked you. To make this process more effective, you want to stay in the mainstream. Staying in the mainstream can be tricky.

How do you become informed about what is going on in the market? Start by reading. There are many sources of information that will help you to figure out where the work is flowing. National, international, regional, and local news sources are important, as are those tied to your trade. For example, I encourage clients to read national news sources such as the *Wall Street Journal* and *New York Times*. For Chicago-based clients, I suggest the *Chicago Tribune* and *Crain's Chicago Business*, and resources for lawyers such as *American Lawyer*, the *ABA Journal*, *Chicago Lawyer*, the *Chicago Daily Law Bulletin*, and blogs. Note that website ads on related sites and job sites for lawyers generally indicate where the market is more active, as the businesses wouldn't spend advertising money otherwise.

When you read about what is going on in the world with an eye toward where the work is, you always want to think about how the information you learn might impact your practice area and how you might utilize this knowledge to enhance your chances for landing a job. You want to think ahead about how work might flow in one direction or another in the future based on these developments. When reading local news for the legal community, be sure to look at the "people in the news" sections. This is where you might read about a litigation practice group splitting off from a large firm and opening its doors as a boutique, or a firm from New York opening a branch in St. Louis. Maybe this new firm could use your help if they have sufficient work-flow. You could talk with people to

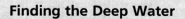

Finding the Deep Water

Two summers ago our family went on a cruise to Alaska. When the ship docked at one of the towns near a river, there was an opportunity to take a rafting trip down the river. Our family signed up to go rafting along with many others from the cruise. When we arrived at the starting point, we were assigned to sturdy, inflated rafts that seated eight. The rafts had guides who told the passengers how and when to paddle and how to shift their weight to help the raft keep moving down the river. These directions were important at the time, because a recent drought meant that there was far less water flowing down this river than there had been in past summers. If we didn't work as a team and follow the guide's directions to keep the raft in the deeper water, it was likely to run aground.

As we started off, we quickly learned that the shallow water was everywhere and that the rocks and pebbles in the shallows would ground the boat. To get the boat moving again, everyone in the raft had to bounce up and down and urge the raft forward to get it off of the shoals. Time and time again the rafts around us ran aground, and we saw the passengers bumping up and down to urge their rafts off of the rocks and pebbles. Our guide was particularly good at keeping our raft in deep water. When I asked him how he did it, he told me that he had been guiding trips down this river for many years and that he knew where the water ran deeper. He had "studied up" on the river.

This is a good analogy for job search in a time of economic uncertainty. With lots of shallow water out there, your job is to "study up" on where the work is flowing. You want to be informed about what is happening in the world generally as well as locally. This keeps your career raft in deeper water.

determine whether the new group is currently busy, active, and growing, but you can also benefit by coming to the attention of the newly created workplace even in the early stages of its development so that you have planted a seed that could grow into a job possibility if and when the group does get busier.

Here is an example of how this sort of information can improve your job quest luck.

One of my clients was a new law school graduate with enhanced knowledge in the health care field. She had a certificate in health care from her law school, won an award for excellence in health law regulation, wrote for the school's health law journal, and was a board member of the Health Law Institute. She read an article in the legal newspaper about two of the smaller local health law boutiques winning a ten-year contract to do work for the National Institutes of Health in an area of the law she had researched for one of her professors. She realized that she should try to maximize her networking efforts with respect to these two firms, even though neither firm seemed to be looking to hire anyone.

As part of her effort, she called the professor she had assisted, who had really liked her work for him on his project, and told him about her interest in these two firms. As "luck" would have it, he knew one of the partners at one of the firms named in the article and was happy to call his friend to put in a good word for her. She was able to land a job at this firm as a result. Clearly, this search strategy based on market knowledge and proactive networking increased her chances for that job. She made good use of one of the wizards from her roundtable to find this opportunity.

Step Four: Create a Master List of People and Places You Want to Explore

Your job quest will advance if you talk in depth with your contacts. You want to develop a *master list of people and places*—people you would like to meet and places that you want to know more about, which you will talk about with your contacts. You grow this list as your search progresses. Throughout your search, you should show this list to anyone you know even tangentially connected with the neighborhood or village you are trying to join. It is important to learn something about the castles that could be a good fit, and the knights and wizards who work there. Ask your contacts, "Do you know any of these people and if so, are they *helpful people* or *nice guys*? What, if anything, do you know about these workplaces?" Even if your contacts may not be associated with the castle you're interested in, it doesn't hurt to share the list. You may discover that your contact knows a knight, wizard, or other castle personnel through other associations.

Which people go on your master list?

➤ People doing the work you think you want to do
➤ People in the neighborhood you are trying to join
➤ People connected to the castles you are trying to vet

Grow the Master List

You have been learning about what is happening in the legal neighborhood where you'd like to live and therefore have some sense of where the work is flowing. You may have read a number of articles that report that some large castles are losing certain practice groups and that the groups have moved to midsize castles. Maybe you have read an article written by a consultant that reflects this trend and predicts more of the same. As a result, you make an educated guess that some midsize firms might be willing to hire if they are trying to grow certain practice groups. You research the midsize firms that could be interested in you given your core competencies, using Google or some other search engine. Next, you go to their websites and research the backgrounds of the individual lawyers who work there. You discover that your background is similar to the backgrounds of other lawyers who work at a number of these targeted firms. By doing this research, you are finding the castles where you might have a good fit and the knights and wizards you would like to talk with. You might also see postings for positions for lawyers, which is often a good sign. This castle needs help and is actively hiring. They are likely to have instructed their dragons to let more résumés past them. If the workplace does not have dragons at the gate, the castle staff might welcome your inquiry especially if you come to their attention through a trusted contact. This is useful information for your quest. As you learn of good prospects this way, be sure to add them to your master lists.

What places go on the list?

➤ Places that could be a good fit for your skill set and background
➤ Places you learn about that are rumored to be busy and may be growing
➤ Places that your research indicates could be getting more work soon
➤ Places where your skill set could transfer and be valuable

Start with what you learn from your research. Even after you embark on your job quest, you will continue to uncover more information about the people and places in the neighborhoods you seek to join. Magazine articles from a wide variety of sources can be very helpful as you try to learn about the people and places that could be good matches for you. Martindale-Hubbell can be useful also. Many cities have directories of practicing lawyers that list where they are working (for example, Sullivan's Law Directory in Chicago). There are also social networking sites such as LinkedIn that can be used to assist your search for specific people in the right neighborhoods. To learn about in-house counsel, the Directory of Corporate Counsel can be helpful. Using Google or other search engines to find the backgrounds of those people who are important for your search can be one of the easiest ways to learn about people and places to add to your master list.

The master list of people and places is important for your search because it will be a focal point for your networking discussions. Instead of talking about jobs, you want to talk about people and places: where the market is stronger, which places are busy and growing, and other information about what is happening in the neighborhood you want to join.

Even if you do not mention the "J" word (talk immediately about jobs), the idea that you are looking for a job is obvious. You need not mention that you are looking for a job, because it is evident from the topic of conversation. You are not putting your contact person on the spot by asking him or her to help you find a job or give you a job. If there is, in fact, a need for someone with your background at the castle where this contact is connected and if you have made a good impression and created trust, this contact person will be quietly vetting you for a job even without being directly asked by you to do so.

Step Five: Learn the Formula for Landing Jobs

When lawyers I am working with come into my office and say four key things, I know it is highly probable that they will land a job. This is the *formula for landing a job*, and it has four elements:

1.   Your *skill set matches* the needs of the workplace or is close enough to answer their need.
2.   You have come to the attention of the workplace through a *trusted contact*—especially one inside the castle or one who is good friends with the keeper of the keys. (Note: Recruiters with good relationships with castle staff also fit this description and can be *trusted contacts*.)

3. The workplace has good *work-flow*.
4. The *music* is good between you and the people in the castle you would be working with. You hit it off with them in an informal interview, or a formal meeting, or a chance meeting. You have a background that matches well with others at that workplace, such as similar schools, mutual friends, or comparable skills.

Use this formula for landing jobs to guide your search efforts. Try to make these four elements happen for you as you conduct your search.

First, target castles that are likely to welcome you. That requires that you do good research on the Internet and in your conversations with contact people. You are looking for workplaces where:

> Your core competencies match their needs; or your skill set is close enough to the needs of the workplace that you can make the argument that you can do the work that needs to be done with a fairly shallow learning curve. You can often figure this out by talking with people who have worked at this castle in the recent past, by checking the website of the castle to learn the backgrounds of people currently working there, finding them on LinkedIn or using Google or another search engine to look up the work history of people at this workplace.

> The workplace is busy and growing and has work that needs to be done. You can figure this out by talking with people. As you conduct your quest you will be talking with knights and wizards to find out whether people at this workplace are busy. Are the lawyers who work there talking about new matters coming in? Are they complaining about how many hours they are working? Are they excited about a new client with a lot of work for the firm? Another source of workflow information can be found in articles in the local online sources, blogs and legal magazines. A partner who is interviewed for an article about the rise of midsize firms might reveal the firm's plan to attract new business by using a different fee structure that corporations have been requesting, and mention that the approach has resulted in a flood of work from certain companies, for example.

> Your personal background seems to be a good match for the workplace. When compared with the others who work there, their backgrounds look like yours in terms of academic institutions, prior workplaces, and experiences and interests. If someone you know and like has joined this workplace and likes it, it is likely

that the "music" will be good for you too. Once you find people who work at a particular castle you think is a good match, you can learn about their backgrounds by using Google or another search engine, or LinkedIn. If you can locate someone who has recently worked there or knows someone who worked there, you can learn about their experiences at this workplace by contacting the person by phone, introducing yourself and asking if the person would be willing to speak with you in confidence about his or her impressions of the workplace. This approach works best with people who no longer are affiliated with that castle and have less incentive to sugar coat their comments. It also works best if you have a friend or trusted contact who introduces you to the person who worked there in the past.

➤ You come to the attention of the key people at the workplace through people they trust.

The last element is the one that requires you to create trust relationships in the neighborhood you are trying to connect with and to utilize your current trust relationships to launch that effort. If you can come to the attention of the workplace through a mutually trusted contact, your chance for landing a job there is greatly enhanced. Even if there is no current opening, when one develops, you are more likely to land it if you are on their radar screen and there is a positive buzz about you with the keeper of the keys and other influential castle personnel.

Step Six: Articulate Your Dream and Dilemma

As you talk with contact people, it is important to help your contacts to help you. The people you meet who are willing to assist you often do not know how to do that effectively. It is your job to instruct them and guide them so that they can provide the information that you need. How do you do that?

Tell your contacts *your dream and your dilemma*. You can also use the words *goal* and *problem*, or *objective* and *difficulty*. If you can clearly define your goal and your problem for your contacts, they will have an easier time knowing how to help you.

How can you identify your dream, objective, and goal? Use your Essential Elements analysis to identify positions and practice areas that you think could be a good match for you. If you have trouble doing this, then you need to talk with people in the field doing the work you think you might want to do to see if their experiences support your educated guesses about what it would be like to work in their job. By talking with people who already do the work you think you want to do and using your template from your Essential Elements exercise, you will be able to find good matches. Once you have done that, you can create a *prototype* for the kind of job that you would like to have.

What is a prototype? Your goal is to find a job, but not just any job. You want to be specific and clear. You should create prototypes or illustrations that are reminiscent of an ad that clearly define the type of position you think would be a good fit for your skills and background and the type of work that exists in the market. Here are some examples:

> "I am looking for a position with a small respected litigation boutique that is busy, active and growing, where people like to work. So I am searching for places that fit that description, whether or not they are currently advertising. Do you know of places that fit that description? And if you do, do you know of any nice people who work there who might talk with me so that I can learn more about that workplace and others that are similar?"

The key word is "nice." Everyone knows who is nice and who is not nice. If you find the nice people in the world you are finding the knights and the wizards who will help you.

> "I am looking for midsize companies that are busy and growing and that may not have in-house counsel. Do you know of other lawyers who are in-house at midsize companies who might be nice enough to talk with me so I can learn more about this market?"

The prototype you provide helps your contact to identify the right group of places to consider and talk about with you. If the prototype is overly specific, however, the contact person might have trouble identifying many possible places that fit the description. You want to create an ad that is specific enough to prompt your contact to identify workplace possibilities but not so specific that you eliminate too many options.

Articulating your dilemma or problem is important also. You need help to solve your problem, and the contact person is in a position to be helpful to you by providing information.

"I am having trouble finding people who do this kind of work, because I just don't travel in those circles. Can you think of good organizations to join? Can you think of good trade journals or blogs or websites to go to so I can read more? Can you think of nice people you know doing the kind of work I want to do?"

"I am having difficulty finding out about these smaller companies and firms because they are not large enough to be written about in *American Lawyer* or known to recruiters and career services has limited information about these companies and firms as well. I need to talk with people who know something about this small company market because they work in a small company, for example. I could use help finding these people. Do you know anyone nice who is doing this kind of work who would take the time to teach me more about this business community?"

Before you launch your quest, be prepared to discuss your goal and your problem. When you articulate your goal and problem for your contact people, the people you meet will be far more helpful to you.

Step Seven: Create a To Do List

You have been identifying people and places that will be part of your quest. You have been learning about organizations that are part of the neighborhood you will be trying to join. You have been identifying magazines, websites, and other sources of information you should read.

To figure out where to begin your journey, think in terms of assigning yourself activities.

The self-assigned work is your to do list. This is simply a list of things you need to do to move your search effort in the right direction. Once you have the list you can start with any item. You work your way through the list item by item. In the process you will be learning more about the neighborhood you want to join and the people you need to meet with. You will add new names of people you need to have lunch with to the "to do" list. This is one of the ways you will grow you master list of people and places. You will assign yourself meetings to go to and blogs to read. The items on your list will change as your search teaches you what you need to do and who to talk with.

A very simple way to begin your list is to write down everyone you know well who is even tangentially connected to the neighborhood(s) you are targeting. Write down every bar association or other kind of group you should check out. Write down journals or blogs or articles you need to read, each on a separate line. Put a box in front of every line item. Then start right in, checking off the boxes as you go. Keep developing the master lists from the knowledge you gain. Everything you do, everyone you talk with, everything you read advances your quest.

There is one last issue to be considered before you walk out the door, and that is your emotional readiness to undertake this adventure.

Step Eight: Do a Mental Status Check

Before you set out on your journey, be sure you are not carrying excess emotional baggage that could weigh you down. Unpack those bags before you start your quest, if at all possible. Sometimes negative emotional baggage can stop you from ever getting out the door at all to conduct your job search. It takes energy to conduct an in-person job search. If you never get out the door, you will miss out on the most important aspect of the networking search, showing up in person, which is crucial for developing trust relationships. If you fail to manage strong negative emotions, those powerful feelings can interfere with and detract from your interview. Depression, anger, resentment, or other negative feelings can cause you to be seen by those you network with as bitter, sarcastic, or depressed, making you a poor choice for their workplace team.

I recently worked with a third-year associate in outplacement, Anne (not her real name). She had been let go by her firm after logging more hours than any of the other associates in her practice group the preceding year. She was considered to be a star performer by many of the partners in her group who entrusted their work to her. Anne had not even considered the possibility that she might lose her job until it happened to her. She thought her position with the firm was secure because so many partners relied on her, she was well liked, and she was the top biller in her associate class. When she was laid off, I received a call from one of the partners who had worked closely with her. Since I was Anne's outplacement coach, the partner was calling to tell me what a wonderful lawyer and person this associate was, how much she had contributed to the practice group, and how much she would be missed by the partners she had worked with. She was the last associate they expected to be fired. The partner who called was also worried about Anne because she was so emotionally upset about being outplaced.

When I met with Anne it was obvious how upset she felt. Her eyes were bloodshot from bouts of crying. She was close to tears throughout our first conversation. She apologized for being so upset. She said she could not believe that this had happened to her. This was the first time in her life that she had failed at anything. She could not understand why the firm had let her go, because she had done everything right and worked extremely hard. She had given up much of her personal life to meet the expectations of her partners, and she had been told that she had been the standout associate in her class, most likely to succeed at the firm. We talked about the unfairness of this situation and how she was justified to be as upset as she was.

As we worked together in our sessions, it was clear to me that Anne was a bright, capable lawyer, just as her partner had described her to be. It was likely that she would land on her feet, but only if she could manage her emotions. Anne and I needed to address her emotional state. I encouraged her to talk about her feelings and passed her a large box of tissues. After a period of time, however, I suggested that her tears might be her way of expressing a pretty intense anger. That was an idea she could use. It was a turning point for her. After that she was able to divert the energy she had been putting into her sadness into more productive activities. For Anne, it was helpful to recognize that she was enraged about what happened to her and that her feelings were justified. After that she used her anger to motivate her search. No longer weepy, she felt more empowered and got to work finding a better job.

Anne had one of the fastest job searches I have ever witnessed. Her search lasted just over one month. She landed a good job at a litigation boutique. Part of her success was the result of her strong desire to do whatever she could to work hard on her search. Because she had been such a standout at her past firm, she had a group of enthusiastic partners who were ready and willing to assist her and endorse her when she asked for their help.

The key to overcoming destructive emotional baggage triggered by difficult circumstances, such as being fired, is to talk about your feelings with someone you trust. The person needs to be able to listen to you without telling you what you should feel or trying to get you to pretend you do not feel what you are experiencing. The person listening should not be judgmental.

How can you find such a person? Sometimes it is possible to find a job search partner who is struggling with the same or similar feelings. If you attend a support group for lawyers, you might meet someone you could pair up with for mutual support. Talking with a truly unbiased, supportive person can help you to recover your sense of equilibrium. Some people use meditation effectively to deal with difficult situations and clear their heads. For others, exercise can help. Still others might take up boxing or karate. There are many ways to let off steam and regain balance.

Most good therapists or counselors will be able to help you with this short-term goal as well. Professional counselors will support you and allow you to express difficult feelings. If, however, you experience a serious depression, which could include thoughts of suicide, plans to carry out a suicide, sleepless nights that do not abate, loss of appetite, or an inability to function during the day, it is important to seek help from a qualified mental health professional.

Turning to alcohol or drugs to get relief from bad feelings only masks the pain. It will not solve underlying emotional issues and can make your life a lot worse if your use becomes a habitual way of trying to cope.

It is important to learn to manage uncomfortable feelings, identify underlying emotions such as anger and helplessness, confront fears of humiliation or other fears, and deal with self-doubt. This is all part of the quest you are on. Often, it is our own personal sense of failure or humiliation that we ascribe to others that prevents us from conducting an effective interpersonal search. We assume other people think badly of us, when, in fact, we are our own harshest critics. And, for every person who does judge you harshly for getting fired or wanting to change to a new practice area, or jumping from one job to another, there are more people who will understand, who have faced something similar, and who will support you. Part of the quest you are on is to find these folks, to join their ranks and help them out too.

If you are able to begin your quest with personal strength and resilience, this attitude will help you get luckier. Bad things happen to everyone in life. The way we handle our misfortune can and often will affect our future success. Figure out how to find treasure in the trash. You will be more capable, energetic, aware of nuances that aid your judgment, and able convey a more positive and powerful image if you can unpack your emotional baggage before you go out the door.

5 How to Start Your Quest

You have done your preparation, and now you are ready to go out the door of your cottage, enter the forest, and look for knights and wizards who will help you find your way to the castles you think could be good for you. What you will discover when you enter the woods is that the forest is full of people who can and will help you. These are the knights and the wizards. You will also encounter a handful of people who will not be helpful. These are the ogres. You need to be ready to talk with the people you meet by

- *Knowing how to spot knights, wizards, and ogres.*
- *Using the starter conversation to find natural counselors.*
- *Using the voice test to determine the knights and wizards from the ogres.*
- *Encouraging knights and wizards to meet with you in person.*

Who Are the Knights and Wizards?

In the most elementary terms, knights and wizards are the natural counselors of the world. They are people who enjoy helping, advising, and mentoring other people. They are people who are engaged with other people and are willing to assist others.

45

Knights and wizards are *nice people*. That may seem like an overly simplistic way to describe someone you are looking for, but it turns out to be the best way to find the right people to help you. Everyone knows who is nice and who is not. Asking "Who do you know at that workplace/ committee/group who is a nice person?" or "Who do you know who might be nice enough to take the time to talk with me?" turns out to be one of the most effective ways to find helpful people.

Wizards, like knights, are helpful to others *and* they are also particularly well positioned and knowledgeable about the castles and the villages surrounding them. They are especially valuable because they possess even greater information and power than some of the knights. The reason they have even more power to help you is that they are very well connected in the community you are trying to join. Wizards tend to be more senior, usually in their 40s, 50s, or 60s. They have created many trust relationships in the villages they inhabit. They may have been college classmates with people who are now the managing partners at law firms and well-positioned in-house counsels. They may go on fishing trips or ski trips with the gatekeepers and the key keepers in the legal community you are trying to connect with. They may have children in the same school or serve on boards with members of the castle staff. Even after people leave the workforce and retire, there is still a period of time when they maintain connections into the vital center of a legal neighborhood.

Many new graduates hesitate to ask their parents or their parents' friends to help them with their job searches, but it is a mistake to exclude anyone who could be a wizard from assisting you with your quest.

Who Are the Ogres?

Ogres, on the other hand, are not going to help you, and sometimes they can interfere with your quest by damaging your motivation and attitudes about your job search. Do not be surprised when you meet ogres on your journey. Every adventure has to have a few challenges. Instead of retreating to the safety of your cottage, try to think about ogres differently so that you can continue your quest.

The ogres of the world are people who generally avoid helping others, not just you. Many of them are having a tough time in life. You might never learn why someone has become an ogre but there could be important reasons for his or her behavior. Perhaps the person has cancer and has not admitted that to anyone else yet. Maybe this person is introverted and never learned to relate well to other people. Maybe the person is getting a divorce, which is causing a lot of personal stress. You may never learn why a person has gone to the "dark side," but there could be an underlying reason. If you meet an ogre, the best approach is to try to be forgiving. Do not let an encounter with an ogre stop you from your quest. Keep looking for the knights and the wizards and have faith that you will find them. Ask the ogres if they know someone helpful, nice, or supportive who would spend time talking with you. Even ogres know who the knights and wizards are in their neighborhood.

It is also possible that someone who seems at first to be a knight or wizard could turn into an ogre during your conversation.

A good illustration of an encounter with an ogre who seemed, at first, to be a knight or wizard, comes from a woman I worked with recently. Her story also illustrates the power of an ogre to damage a job seeker's attitude about her job search.

Ginger graduated from a top-tier law school where she had done well academically. She found a job as an associate at a high-powered law firm after graduation from law school. At first she enjoyed the work, but after a few years, she felt burned out and stressed out by the pace and demands of the job. She left the firm to do contract work. After about a year of contract work, she felt ready to return to an associate position with a firm on track for partnership once again or go in-house. However, at this point there were fewer opportunities with large or midsize firms because of a rocky economy. The only jobs she could find were more contract positions. This work was not satisfying for her. She wanted more of a challenge.

Ginger went to a conference to hear about other options in the law, and attended a panel discussion about in-house jobs for lawyers. One of the speakers was an in-house counsel who spoke about options for lawyers at her level of practice. After the panel discussion was over and the speakers were preparing to leave, Ginger approached the panelist.

At first he was very friendly and asked about her background. When he heard the law school she graduated from and the first firm where she had worked, he became very interested and conversational. She then gave him her résumé and he reviewed it. When he saw that she was currently doing contract work, his attitude abruptly shifted. He became negative and scolded her, saying, "No wonder you are having trouble finding good work. You should never have left your job for a contract position." After that sharp comment to her, he got very busy with his papers and essentially ended the conversation. Ginger was devastated, and after that, she shied away from networking until we met for counseling.

The panelist had certainly appeared to be a knight, or even a wizard, but he turned out to be an ogre. Ginger felt at least temporarily defeated by his comments and she let the incident interfere with her networking efforts for a period of time. It wouldn't be a heroic quest without a villain or two to deal with. In *Star Wars* Luke Skywalker had to contend with Darth Vader, but that did not stop him from his quest. Don't let the ogres of the world deter you from your mission.

Fortunately, knights and wizards are more plentiful—anecdotally, based on the reports from my clients, I'd estimate that two thirds of the people you'll meet are knights and wizards, and only one third are ogres. In addition, knights and wizards are easy to spot using the Voice Test on page 56. Your job is to find more helpful people, because your search progresses as you go from one helpful person to another. That is how you get over the mountain, through the forest, and make it to the castles.

Who Are the Gatekeepers?

Every workplace has people who can help you get past the castle gates. They have the ability to get a job seeker recognized in the inner sanctum of the castle by the keeper of the keys or other important castle staff. The gatekeepers sometimes do not realize that they have this power. They might just work in the castle or have a relationship with the castle's key keeper or someone else trusted by the key keeper, and because there is no official recognition of the role of gatekeeper, they may not think they have any power whatsoever. Sometimes a gatekeeper is a husband, wife, or other relative of someone inside the castle, for example. Sometimes the gatekeeper works in a related castle or plays golf or is on a board with a key keeper. For that reason, if you ask that person to take your résumé to the person in charge of hiring, the response might be, "Sure, but I don't know if that will do any good."

It is important for you as a job seeker to recognize that, even if the gatekeeper is unsure of her clout, she might still be more of a trusted contact than she recognizes. So, ask the gatekeeper to introduce you to someone in the castle hierarchy if you know that the introduction will be positive. And coach the gatekeeper to help you by saying something good about you to those in the castle hierarchy if it is appropriate to do so. You are asking for an *endorsement.* But be careful to ask for that only if it is appropriate.

An endorsement has the following three elements:

> ➤ Your contact knows you, likes you, and knows your work (work product and work ethic).
> ➤ Your contact knows someone in the castle hierarchy who is approachable and nice.
> ➤ You know that the workplace could be in need of the kind of help you could provide.

If this gatekeeper you know asks, "Do you want me to say a good word about you when I talk with my friend (the key keeper)?" your answer is "yes." Endorsements are very powerful and helpful from people who are respected and trusted by those inside the castle. Endorsements help to transfer the trust that the people in the workplace have in the contact person, to you, the as yet unknown job seeker.

Some people are well versed in the ways of networking and will need no coaching to volunteer positive comments about you. Other people are not as aware of the power of a few positive words to transfer trust. Endorsements are so important that it is better not to leave to chance whether your gatekeeper will say something positive about you when he or she introduces you to the castle hierarchy.

You never want to aggressively push anyone to give you an endorsement, however. Instead, say something that gives the gatekeeper the option to decline. For example, you might say, "I do not want you to feel pressured to do this, but if you are comfortable doing it, I would really appreciate it if you would say something positive to your friend X about my integrity, my work ethic, or anything else you have liked about my work with you on that committee we served on together."

In this way you signal your gatekeeper that you would like support, but you also offer a gracious way to decline if it is too uncomfortable for your contact person to take that role. By modeling the comment you are looking for from your contact person, you also help that person construct a productive endorsement that will open a door for you. Be certain that if you are asking your contacts to vouch for your work, they know your work product. Without that knowledge, they can only say you are likeable, which is a weaker testimonial.

Where Will You Find Knights and Wizards?

Join the legal community and become a participant. Meet with people who live in the neighborhood you want to join. In the context of your job quest, think of the legal community or neighborhood that you are trying to connect with as the village behind the castle where tradesmen and tradeswomen interact with each other and also know the folks who live in the castle. You want to show up there and become known to them. You also need to learn more about who lives in that neighborhood.

At times you might feel as if you have become something of a "groupie," learning who is a standout in the legal neighborhood and who is contributing to the group even though you might currently be an outsider. You also want to learn about the hot topics for this practice area. What are lawyers talking about? You can learn a lot of this information by reading local business magazines and legal publications, participating in bar association committees, and checking bulletins for events scheduled by the bar associations in that practice area.

You can also talk with the lawyers who live in the village or who are traveling through the forest. As you find your way through the woods, advancing from trusted contact to trusted contact, you will meet new knights and wizards by being introduced to them by knights and wizards you already know.

What Is a Starter Conversation?

A *starter conversation* is one in which you reach out to your contacts or to people your contacts suggest you connect with or to a possible knight or wizard you have encountered to see if they will be helpful to you. It is important for the success of your search that you have a great many starter conversations.

One of the best ways to do this is by making a telephone call to someone you think is in any way connected to the castle or the village behind

How to Meet Knights and Wizards

One of my clients, a forty-year-old dissatisfied transactional real estate partner at a small firm, decided he wanted to make a fairly radical career shift into what was, at the time, the new field of information technology. He needed to learn the practice area in order to enhance his value to this new market. So he enrolled in an LL.M. program (Master of Laws) in information technology. As part of his job search, we mapped out his strategy. One step was to get involved at the local bar association and very actively participate in the relatively new IT committee.

He got involved with that newly formed committee, set up committee programs, and created relationships with the panelists as he put together those meetings. He also co-authored a cutting-edge paper in the field of IT with one of his professors. In the process of getting involved in this legal community and creating a presence for himself, he was referred to potential clients, groups of young entrepreneurs with start-up companies who needed legal help but did not have a lot of money. The referrals came from his professor and from some of the more established lawyers he met who were involved in the bar committee. One of the entrepreneurial groups he counseled developed rapidly into a successful business and, following the career plan he had set up, he proposed himself as their in-house counsel. He prepared a business proposal and made a presentation to the company. When they accepted, he was thrilled. He had done what few lawyers are able to do late in a career, transition laterally out of one practice area into a totally different area and land an in-house counsel position with an exciting new business in only about a year's time.

If you can find a way to interact with the community you want to join, you will enhance your luck, especially if you create a positive buzz about yourself in the neighborhood.

the castle. The person you contact may not work in the castle but may be married to someone whose cousin works in the castle. The person you contact may be retired and no longer live in the village behind the castle, but only two years ago had many contacts in that village and still has some good information about who is important there and which workplaces might be thriving.

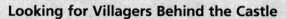

Looking for Villagers Behind the Castle

An example of finding gatekeepers to promote a job quest for a government position comes from a client who was a litigation associate at a large firm. He had graduated from a top-tier law school with excellent grades and had been an editor for law review. After graduation he went to a law firm where he was assigned to the litigation group. He was expected to be an aggressive and confrontational lawyer when he was more of a reasonable, thoughtful person by nature. Appellate work, with its emphasis on research, writing, and oral argument, was far more enjoyable for him.

In our work together it became clear that a career move into a position with the federal government might be a good strategic and personal career decision for him. He looked at usajobs.gov, the website for federal employment, and learned of a number of job prospects that fit with his interests in appellate-based work. He prepared his applications.

He then launched his quest for classmates who were working for the federal government. One day while he was looking at one of the websites for one of the federal agencies he was interested in, he thought he saw in the background of one of the workplace photos the somewhat blurred image of a classmate from law school. He contacted his friend by e-mail and sure enough, his friend was working at that agency. When he told his friend about his interest in a job at the same agency, his friend told him to shoot his résumé over and he would hand deliver it to the person in charge of hiring. That is what my client did, and within about two weeks he was asked to come to Washington, D.C., for an interview. He was hired by the agency a few weeks later and continues to be very happy with that decision.

You could say it was lucky that he saw his friend in the photo, but it is more accurate to conclude that he created his good luck by looking for people he knew in the village behind the castle and maximizing the chance when he did find someone. In addition, since he was a nice guy himself, who was known to people in his law school in a positive way, he was able to get an endorsement from a friend who was connected to the keeper of the castle keys.

Finding Gatekeepers in a New City

Another of my clients, Dorothy (not her real name), was a midlevel associate who did insurance defense. She had been vacillating about whether to leave her law firm in the Midwest and move to Arizona. Her firm expected associates to work long hours and assigned a heavy volume of work but offered little chance of eventual partnership. She was burned out doing insurance defense and wanted to change practice areas. To make matters even more challenging, the recession was in full swing at the time she was trying to make this decision.

Still, Dorothy went through the process of finding her career sweet spot and she identified commercial litigation as a practice area that she was more excited about. Dorothy learned how to conduct a job quest, prepared a new résumé, and practiced her interview. But since she had no connections in Arizona, Dorothy continued to be indecisive about whether to leave her current job and risk a move. One day she came into my office and told me that she was sick and tired of being ambivalent. She had decided. She would quit her job and do what she had wanted to do for many years. Dorothy applied to take the Arizona bar exam, sold her condo, quit her job, rented a van, and moved to Phoenix.

I did not hear from Dorothy for many months. When I heard from her, I was delighted to learn that she had made a successful transition. She sent me this e-mail:

> I wanted to update you on my progress since moving to Phoenix at the end of February and thank you for your guidance in my job search! I will start work at P__ on Monday doing business/commercial litigation. I am thrilled about the job. I got out of insurance defense in this market . . . I employed your strategy for networking and getting interviews, and I think it was a great success, thank you! I had several connections here that I could exploit and, to your point, there were many people who were willing to meet in person and help out. I got a lot of mileage out of a few meetings. It was easy to be positive about the search after having helpful people on board with my searching and making calls became easier over time. One place I interviewed laughed because I knew so many people around town (thanks to your method) and that I had people from all over advocating for me—even on the golf course!

Learning how to connect with people who might be able to advance your search is a challenge that forms the basis for the productive networking search. One of the best ways to do this is to have a lot of starter conversations that pave the way for you to advance your mission. Dorothy's success was based in part on her willingness to have many starter conversations after moving to Phoenix.

Call the contact and engage in the following conversation.

First, introduce yourself and give your connection to the person you are calling. The connection needs to be either a person in common or an experience you share. You never want to make a cold call.

If it's a person in common it can sound like this:

"Hi, my name is Sam and I am a friend of Scott Davis. Scott suggested that I call you and said you'd be a really helpful person to ask for advice and information. I hope I am not calling you at a bad time, but if I am please let me know. I would be happy to set up a time to call back later."

If you have an experience in common, it might sound like this:

"Hi, my name is Sam and I don't know if you remember me, but we were on the same bar association committee" (went to the same law school or same undergrad school, have kids in an activity together, belong to the same club . . .).

The rule of thumb is that if you had some sort of friendship or working relationship in the past that satisfied the threshold level of friendship, it is usually fine to assume those people will remember you in a positive way, especially if you remember them in a positive way as well.

Second, tell the person about why you are calling (your dilemma/problem).

"I am at a crossroads in my career."

"I am trying to figure out some things having to do with my career."

"I am trying to learn about what is going on in certain legal markets."

The key words and phrases to use: advice, information, market knowledge, insights; "I am hoping you will brainstorm with me." You can add: "And, by the way, I am *not* calling to ask you for a job."

Third, give the person a glowing synopsis of your background. This is your résumé. Say good things about yourself. And be succinct. Even your best friends do not really know what you do, so you have to give each contact a snapshot of your skill set and experience. You can say, "I hope you don't mind if I tell you a little bit about myself so that you are in a better position to advise me."

Fourth, describe what you are looking for (your castles). This is where you put your workplace prototype to use. The prototype is your description of the types of workplaces that you have determined would be a good fit for you given your skills and the market need.

> "I am looking for small respected firms doing mostly estate planning and consulting to wealthy families."

> "I am looking for small, respected litigation boutiques."

> "I am looking for midsize companies that do not have in-house counsel and currently use outside counsel for their legal work."

Then always add, "I am interested in places that are busy, active, growing, and have a good reputation, meaning that people like working there."

In other words, you are trying to find the castles for which you have written a prototype, and you are asking your contact to help you to identify the places that fit the description(s).

Fifth, ask people to turn on their mental computers. If you have more than one type of workplace that would be good for your skill set and career goals, then walk your contact through the description of each one. Do this methodically, one by one. You never know who your contact person knows, so do not presume to know that the person can only connect you with one type of village or castle.

Even if the information you are seeking could be obtained via Google or some other resource on the Internet, do not go that route. These interactions lay the groundwork for relationships that are crucial for your networking success and for success in marketing in the future. As people assist you, you create *friendship lite* opportunities and trust relationships.

At this juncture you are hoping that the contact person will identify places that fit the description of the workplace you are looking for. If you have done your homework, you may well have heard of these places. If so, see what more you can learn that will advance your search. Your conversation may go something like the following.

> "Can you think of places that fit the description(s) I just gave you?"

> "Have you thought of Steptoe and Forrest? Or how about Johnson and Lewis?"

"Yes, I read about that firm. Didn't they just form last year? I think they broke off from Kirkland and Ellis, didn't they? What do you hear about that workplace? Do you know any of the people over there? Do you know someone nice over there who might be willing to talk with me about the firm and what they do? And would it be ok with you if I use your name to connect with this person to learn more? Or, better yet, if you are comfortable doing it, I would really appreciate it if you sent the person you know an e-mail to explain who I am and what I would be contacting him to talk about. But please be up front about it if you don't feel comfortable introducing me. I will not be upset by that."

Sixth, try to meet in person. At some point in the process of having this conversation, you should try to change the meeting from telephone to in-person. It may be best to do that fairly early in the conversation. The time to transition to an in-person meeting is when you realize you have found a knight or wizard (see the next section, "What Is the Voice Test?"). As a transition, you might say, "I don't know if you have the time to meet with me in person, but the information you are giving me is so useful, so helpful, I wonder if I could buy you a cup of coffee (or meet for breakfast/lunch/dinner or in your office) so we could keep talking. Would you be willing to do that?"

The person will either say yes or no. If it's no, you can continue to talk over the phone. If the person says yes, you have just landed an informal interview. Technically you have landed an informational interview, but the ramifications go beyond that whether you intend them to or not.

What Is the Voice Test?

You can identify a knight or wizard by voice in the first few minutes of your starter conversation. A knight's or a wizard's voice goes up in pitch. An ogre's voice goes down. This is the *voice test.*

When you talk with people who engage with you, you can hear it in their voice. When a person engages with you, he starts to think along with you. He might say, "Oh, you should talk with my friend, Nick"; or, "I know just the person you need to meet!" You can hear that engagement in the pitch and the affect of the voice as well as the content. By contrast, the affect of the ogre is flat and low. "Well, I really don't know who you should talk to. I just don't think I can help you. I just don't know of any jobs." Think of Ben Stein's voice or Eeyore from *Winnie the Pooh*. You can tell the level of engagement from a conversation's content as well.

Because the sound of a person's voice is so important when trying to figure out who the helpful people are, e-mails are not as effective for locating knights and wizards. You cannot hear the affect, pitch, or engagement in the contact's voice in an e-mail exchange. E-mail can, therefore, be misleading or even opaque when it comes to finding natural counselors.

Once You Have Found a Knight or Wizard, What Should You Do?

Meeting in person with the knights and wizards of the world is very important for a successful job quest.

> ➤ On a scale of 1 to 10 with 10 the highest, it is a 10 to meet in person with the natural counselors of the world, the knights, wizards, and gatekeepers. Even if they are simple villagers, lawyers who live in the same neighborhood you are trying to become a part of, they will spread the word about you and help you to become part of the neighborhood buzz.
> ➤ It is a 5 to talk with someone over the phone without any further contact.
> ➤ It is a 3 to communicate only by e-mail.
> ➤ It is a 1 to send something by snail mail when you could be meeting in person.

Why is meeting in person so important? It increases the level of engagement and interaction that is crucial for a productive networking search. The in-person meeting is your chance to really talk with someone who is in the village or connected with the castle. You can hear more of the gossip and rumors. Also, the person cares about you more once you meet face-to-face. You can create greater trust.

The in-person meeting is actually an interview, whether it is billed that way or not. The person who meets with you will, hopefully, go back into the work world and people will talk about you behind your back, which is just what you want them to do. To find a job through the grapevine, you want to become part of the buzz that goes on in the legal work world all the time.

I have a friend who worked in sales for a large company engaged in product development in Japan. Even though Japan is a long way away, he was often in Japan or flying back from Japan when he worked for this company. One day I asked him why he had to travel such a long way so frequently. Why not use videoconferencing to connect with his clients there? He replied, "There is no substitute for shaking someone's hand and looking him in the eye to create trust."

This is true for your job search as well. You are also in sales while you are networking to find a job. You are promoting yourself as a valuable asset. Just as a sales professional needs to show up in person to create trust, in a productive networking search you are creating trust relationships that can help to open doors for you in a number of workplaces. You are also creating trust relationships with many people in the village who then assist you in finding your way to the castles you have described to them. In addition, more magic happens in person. People are memorable, paper is not. By doing your quest in person as much as possible, you are creating and enhancing your own luck.

The Knights of Your Round Table

Part of creating your own good luck is creating a team of people who are advising, supporting, strategizing with, and counseling you. Think of them as the board of directors for your search effort, or the knights who join your round table. If you can find people who will be on your team and are willing to be sources of information and support for you, it can advance your search efforts.

Who do you want on your team? It depends on what you are trying to accomplish in your search and where you are in the arc of your career. If you are a new graduate, you want to enlist your professors, past bosses, partners, or others who have been impressed with your work during your internships or externships. If you are farther along in your career, you should be able to enlist your current bosses, coworkers, past bosses, people you have served on committees with, and others who see you in a positive light.

You will also find new knights for your round table as you create new trust relationships. You want to include people who are connected to your targeted neighborhood, the village where you want to find work, and the castles you are trying to connect with. Career counselors and career services professionals might be good people to add to your team as well. The team you put together will never sit down as a group, of course; they are simply members of a virtual round table that helps you to have a successful quest.

6 How to Get Knights and Wizards to Meet with You

You have begun your adventure. You have entered the forest with an idea of the places you want to explore and the people you want to meet to find your way to the castles.

- *You prepared well.*
- *You are contacting possible knights and wizards by phone.*
- *You are having a lot of starter conversations.*
- *You are using the voice test to find the natural counselors.*
- *You are always approaching a contact through another trusted contact.*

You understand how important it is to meet in person with knights and wizards. But how do you get a busy knight or wizard to meet with you in person?

What Do You Say?

The starter conversation reveals the natural counselors of the world who will engage with you, the knights and the wizards. It also reveals the people who will not engage with you, the ogres. The voice test is the key to that quick determination. Once you make that determination, and you find a knight or a wizard, you know you want to try to meet in person if possible. The more direct and honest you can be, the better, while also being mindful of the contact person's busy schedule.

Here are some examples of how to start:

"I am learning so much from you. I have no idea if you would be willing to meet with me in person, but it would be great if we could do that and keep talking. If you are too busy to do that I understand, but if you could find the time I'd really appreciate it. I'll treat."

"The information you are giving me is so helpful, so useful. Could we get together in person? I'd be happy to meet for breakfast, lunch, dinner, or coffee, or meet at your office. If we go out it's my treat. Whatever works for you."

When Do You Say It?

Within the first few minutes of your starter conversation, you will usually know if the person you are speaking with is or is not engaged with you. If he or she has joined with you to brainstorm, to address your dilemma, to offer suggestions of places and people, that is a good time to try to convert the telephone conversation into an in-person meeting if at all possible. The optimal timing is not something you can pinpoint with perfect accuracy. This is an opportunity to rely on your intuitive judgment and common sense. You should be able to figure out if this person is being helpful or not. Trust your response based on the way that person is interacting with you. The voice test is the single best simple litmus test of another person's connection to your cause. So listen for the voice that goes up in pitch and the affect in the voice to find your knights and wizards.

Why Does This Work?

There are four main reasons why the knights and wizards of the world will agree to meet with you in person.

First, you have been referred through a trusted contact. The positive connection that the contact has with that trusted person transfers to you and paves the way for your connection.

Second, you have used the voice test to find someone who likes advising and counseling others and who gets pleasure and enjoyment out of helping other people. The natural counselors of the world are personally enriched by helping others. The process of assisting another person feels good and brings satisfaction to many people. If you are someone who likes helping others you already know this basic truth. If you are not that kind of person, maybe it's time to re-invent yourself.

Third, the knights and wizards of the world have figured out that networking is a way of life that is important for career success. By helping you out, they are helping themselves out as well. Helping others is ultimately a somewhat selfish thing to do because it engenders a willingness and motivation to repay the favor some day. Maybe you will provide an important business contact. Maybe you will help them find a job some day. If someone has helped you out when you needed that assistance, you will want to give back. What goes around comes around.

Fourth, you have been referred by a friend or business acquaintance of theirs. The contact person wants that business acquaintance to be on good terms. In part the contact person might meet with you as a favor to his friend. The underlying reason matters less than the fact that you have gained access to a knight or wizard. After that it's up to you to make a great impression and learn about what you need to know.

What if They Won't Meet with You?

Sometimes people are just too busy to meet in person. If the contact person is not a close friend or a friend of your close friend, he may be less interested in meeting with you in person. If the contact person is an ogre, you will not meet with him in person. Sometimes, despite your best effort to tell the contact person that you are not going to try to push him to give you a job, the contact person is wary and on guard and may think that you do have that unstated agenda.

If the contact person is not interested in meeting with you face-to-face, or is not able to do so, you can still learn a lot of valuable information over the telephone. If you engage the contact person's help over the phone and then give her something to show you are grateful as well as thank her verbally, you might convince her that you are someone who can be trusted and that you are worth helping. The gifts you can give do not cost you anything other than time. They are gifts of connection, information, promotion, and supportive listening (see Chapter 8, "Friendship Lite"). Whether or not you are able to give your contact person a gift, just thanking her verbally for help may be sufficient. People who are willing to help others are rewarded and gratified when they are asked to take the role of helper as long as the person looking for assistance does so in a thoughtful way. You always want to be mindful of your contact's time constraints and express your gratefulness for any assistance.

What to Avoid Saying and Doing

Once you have found a knight or wizard using the voice test, you know you have found a contact who enjoys engaging with and helping others. You never want to take advantage of someone who is willing to do that. One way you might create a problem for yourself is by becoming a pest —someone who is a recurring problem for the contact person. If you call back repeatedly to ask for advice and information, or if you e-mail constantly for feedback and guidance, you run the risk of losing their support.

You want to elicit the contact person's advice and learn what that person has to offer you, including the names of additional contact people; thank them; give them a simple gift of information, promotion, connection, or other support; and move along on your quest through the woods. Every time you interact with a contact person try to make the interaction beneficial for your contact. Always think about what you could do to make that person's life better in return. You can occasionally circle back with additional questions if they arise and you really need to reconnect, but be careful not to wear out your welcome.

When you engage another person to ask for assistance, it can be a mistake to use a pretense or a bogus reason to set up a meeting. Say, for example, you learn that the person you want to meet with loves horses and owns a horse. You do not know the first thing about horses, but you pretend that you are interested in them and engineer a "chance" meeting at the stable where he keeps his horse. This falls into the category of pretense, and if your lack of knowledge or interest becomes obvious, the ploy will backfire.

However, there can be occasions for creative networking if there is an authentic shared interest. Say, for example, you have done triathlons and plan to do more of them, and you learn that the wizard you are hoping to connect with does them too. If you learn that he is going to be helping to organize and run a 10K event for lawyers, it could be creative networking at its best to volunteer to assist with the management of that event and find an opportunity to meet up with that wizard.

Pretense or dishonesty in your early interactions with contact people can affect the level of trust you gain or lose. Ultimately, the quest is about creating trust relationships and gaining a positive reputation in the community in which you want to live for the rest of your legal career. It is not about gaming the system. The last thing you want to do is create a negative buzz in this neighborhood you want to join. People are smart. Wizards and knights did not get to be wizards and knights without having good instincts. If you are being disingenuous, smart people will usually figure it out and may think less of you for it.

The Confidentiality Issue

If you are conducting a networking search, you might be justifiably concerned that the buzz you create in your legal neighborhood could get back to your current employer. The way to minimize this potential problem is to tell everyone you talk with that you really need to keep this conversation confidential. Say it four times. First, say it at the beginning of your conversation to set up your meeting. Second, say it in the beginning of your conversation in person. Third, say it at the end of your in-person conversation. Fourth, say it in your thank-you e-mail.

What do you say? "I just want you to know that it really could be a problem if my current workplace/boss hears about my search. I really hope you can be extremely careful to maintain confidentiality."

In my practice, clients who have inoculated their networking conversations in this way have not reported a breach of confidentiality. The downside of this approach is that there may be a less expansive buzz created in the legal neighborhood.

On occasion, when a job seeker has voluntarily told his or her employer about doing a job search, the surprising result was that the employer offered a more attractive deal to get the job seeker to stay. This is a situation that requires reliance on your intuitive judgment, including the leverage you have at the workplace and the way coworkers have been treated previously when they conducted job searches at this workplace.

7 What Happens in Meetings with Knights and Wizards

You are on this job quest to find your way to castles your research indicates could be good for you. You are calling your closest knight and wizard friends, and through them you learn about other knights and wizards who will guide you through the forest. You call them and have starter conversations. Some of the people you talk to have agreed to meet with you in person. You want those meetings to go well. These contact people have the potential to

- *Guide you through the forest.*
- *Help you locate other castles.*
- *Tell you where the work-flow is stronger.*
- *Help you fulfill your dream and solve your dilemma.*
- *Help you to meet the castle gatekeepers and key keepers.*
- *Join your round table as a coach and advisor.*

You need to know what to say, what to ask for, and how to help your contacts to help you.

Create a Comfort Zone

You are about to meet in person with a knight or a wizard. You have already had a brief conversation. You have noted over the phone that you are at a crossroads in your career and looking for guidance and information. This person has already started to help you in that brief conversation. You converted the conversation to an in-person meeting and now you are going to have that meeting.

Start with small talk. Talk about neutral subjects like weather or whether the person has ever been to this restaurant before or a mutual friend or a mutual experience or an interesting piece of jewelry that the person is wearing or some other innocuous topic of conversation. You want your contact to feel comfortable talking with you. Start small and look for commonalities.

Even though you are talking with this person in a business context, it is fine to talk about lightly personal things such as family or a strong interest, like golf or some other pursuit that he or she does for fun. There may be a shared interest in a charity or not-for-profit, hiking, or travel. There may be commonalities around where to go for vacation or small talk about holiday plans. None of these topics is overly personal or highly charged. They serve to create a comfort zone for everyone and form the underpinnings of a casual business friendship.

Once you have created that comfort zone, though, you want to move on to some important topics that will help you with your quest.

Start with Biography

Once you have a comfort zone, you can move into a conversation that includes your contact's background. You can ask how your contact got where he is today and learn about his career choices. In the process of hearing someone's story, you can learn a lot about what works and does not work in the context of a career in the same practice area you are interested in. When you learn someone's biography, you hear about this person's way of thinking and his choices and why he did what he did. All of this is valuable information. In addition, you are asking this person to tell you his career story. Most people enjoy doing that.

Ask open-ended questions as you would if you were doing a direct examination of a cooperative witness. For example:

"How did you get into this practice area?"

"What do you like/dislike about it?"

"If you had your career to do over again would you still choose this career path? Why or why not?"

"Who seems to do well in this field? Why do you think that is?"

"Who seems to get ahead at this law firm? Why is that?"

"What do you wish you had known before you started this career?"

"What are five things about this career/job that surprised you?"

Biography can teach you a lot, but you cannot limit the conversation to biography. There is a great deal of ground you want to cover in a short period of time, so it is important to move on from this topic. When do you move the conversation to the subject of your job quest? This is another moment when you rely on your intuitive judgment to guide you.

Talk About Your Dream and Dilemma

Although you want to begin with small talk and biography, you need to move the conversation along so that you can eventually ask for the on-the-ground advice and information about the market and work-flow that you are hoping to gain. One of the best ways to start that phase of the conversation is to say something like this:

> "You sound like you have been able to create a terrific career for yourself in this practice area. I am hoping to be able to do something similar. I have a dream, you could say, and a dilemma (or a goal and a problem). One of the reasons I wanted to meet with you is to tell you my goal and to get your advice about how you would accomplish this goal if you were me, given what you know about the field."

Since you are meeting with someone who is a natural counselor, asking for advice engages your contact in a topic that is likely to be interesting to him.

Be an Investigative Reporter

The best way to conceptualize your role in the in-person meeting at this juncture is to think of yourself as an investigative reporter. Your job is to find out what is going on in the forest and in the castles. You need to find other people to talk with. Investigative reporters are not shy about asking questions that will give them accurate and up-to-the-minute information. They need to get the story, just as you need to. They need to create relationships to get to the next source of information, just as you need to. Here are some questions you might ask:

> Here is my résumé. Where do you think a lawyer with my skill set might be valuable in the current market?
> Do you know of workplaces that are busy and growing? Why do you think they are busy?
> How do people get hired at certain workplaces? (provide the names)
> Do you know who is in charge of hiring at certain workplaces? (provide the names)
> Given my background, do you have any ideas which other workplaces would welcome me?
> In the field right now where do you see the greatest activity? Which lawyers are busy at your firm? Which practice areas?
> Given my goal and problem do you have other ideas for me, other advice?
> Do you know of groups I should join or blogs or other publications I should read?
> I have a list of people I would really like to learn about or meet if I could. Here is that list. Do you happen to know any of these people; and if you do, do you think any of them would be nice guys, willing to talk with me and provide advice and information as you are doing?
> If you do know of more people who are doing the work I would like to be doing, do you think it would be a good idea for me to contact them to learn more? I would not be asking for a job, just to be clear about that.
> I have a list of places that I would really like to learn more about. Here is the list. Do you know what's going on at any of these workplaces?
  • Do you know people who work there or used to work there recently?
  • I'm interested in how they find new hires and who is in charge of hiring, if you know.
  • I'm also interested to learn how busy they are.
> If you think it is a good idea to contact these people, would you be willing to send your friend an e-mail to introduce me so that I won't end up in the spam filter?
> Can you think of anyone else I could talk with to get advice and information on these topics?

As you ask these questions, the answers you get from the contact person will lead to more questions you will want to ask to open up productive areas of inquiry for your search. This is not meant as a definitive list of questions to ask.

Know How to Turn the Meeting into a Job Opportunity

There are some important ways that your mission is different from that of an investigative reporter. Unlike a reporter, the story you are investigating is about you, namely, "How does a lawyer with my skill set and background fit into the current market?" This story has deep personal relevance for you.

In addition, the person you are interviewing is also interviewing you at the same time. The person you are talking with is learning about you and your aspirations and seeing your résumé and advising you. Your contact is learning about what you are looking for and trying to brainstorm with you to figure out where you could find opportunities. Together you are on a mission to help you find the right job.

Your contact knows that your goal is to find job opportunities. Consequently, without ever mentioning *jobs*, this contact person will be considering whether you would be a good fit for her workplace. For this reason, if you do have an interest in the contact's workplace, you should speak up and say so. If you do not say anything, the contact person might conclude that you are interested in other workplaces but not hers. You need to quickly assess whether the contact's workplace sounds interesting to you and whether you truly fit the criteria for landing a job there.

Apply the formula for landing a job:

1. You have the right skill set,
2. The workplace is busy,
3. You come to the attention of the workplace through a trusted contact, and
4. The music is likely to be good between you and the people who work there. Be sure that your background is similar to the backgrounds of lawyers working there.

If you are interested and you do fit the criteria, then speak up. Here is what you can say:

> "I have no idea if your workplace has a need for someone with my background, but as you were talking about where you work it seemed like it might be a pretty good fit. I wonder if it would make sense to talk to whoever is in charge of hiring. Who is that?"

If you find out this information, you have discovered the keeper of the castle keys. Tell your contact that it would be helpful if you could meet with this person. Then ask your contact, "Does that sound like a good idea? Could that be arranged?" If the workplace is relatively small to mid-sized, this may be the way they find their new hires. If you can meet the key keeper even before the workplace has a need to hire someone with your background and you stay in touch with people at that workplace, your chances to land the next job for someone with your background will be far better. You may have successfully recruited yourself to your future workplace.

Help Your Contact Person to Help You

Many job seekers conduct their networking searches by asking everyone they know if they have heard of any jobs rather than by asking for advice and information, trying to meet targeted people in the right neighborhood, sharing their dream and dilemma, and learning where the work-flow is stronger. Consequently, many contact people you encounter will assume that you are only interested in information about current job openings and whether their workplace would want to hire you immediately. As we have seen, however, that leads to a response that is too brief and not helpful enough for your purposes. For that reason, if your contact person says something like," I don't know of any jobs. If I hear of something I will send you an e-mail or call you," be sure to gently redirect him or her to answer the questions you are asking. Try saying something like this:

> "You know, what I am most interested in learning is any on-the-ground information, including speculation and rumors about what is going on in this practice area and this group of firms and companies that need lawyers in this practice area. I do not know enough about the market yet. I need to learn more. I hope I am not imposing on you too much by asking you so many questions."

It is your job to keep your contact person on course, providing you with the information you really need. Help them to help you. Guide them back to your questions, and do not let them end the conversation without learning more of the information you need to have to enhance your luck.

Give Back

Since the information you seek takes time and effort on the part of your contact person, you want to be mindful of that and thank your contact for helping you. Arguably the single most important aspect of your networking search goes beyond landing your job. The most important aspect of your effort to find work is that you create trusted contacts in the neighborhood you want to belong to for the rest of your career. You are creating new friends. These relationships can open doors for future business and future jobs. Some of these people you meet will be on your team, supporting you and helping you find opportunities. Many will become closer friends over time. You owe it to your contacts to assist them too. You want to return the favor if you are able to do so.

How can you do that? Business friendships are not always personal friendships. For example, more senior people who counsel and guide you, the wizards, may not be your peers. How do you help them out, especially if you are just beginning your career? You may not think that you are in a position to give them important information or advice in return. But that is not true. That brings us to the concept of *friendship lite,* which we will explore in the next chapter.

8 Friendship Lite

You are on your job quest meeting with knights and wizards in the forest, finding more helpful people. Even when you encounter an ogre, he can tell you about knights and wizards to contact. You are meeting with these contacts and telling these natural counselors your dream and dilemma, asking for guidance, learning on-the-ground gossip and rumors about the work-flow and places that are busy, active, and growing, and you are showing people your master list of people and places and finding more knights and wizards. These people have taken time out of their busy lives to counsel you. The time they spend with you is not billable. What can you do to thank them for their help? That is what this chapter is about.

What Is Friendship Lite?

The wizard or knight you meet with is a person you have asked for help in a business context. This contact may be a teacher, a current or past boss, a coworker, a person who attended your law school or your undergraduate school, a friend of your father, mother, or other family member, a judge who has seen you at work in court. By using a starter conversation and the voice test, you have uncovered the natural counselors. When you engage the help of a natural counselor, you are creating a relationship. The relationship may or may not evolve into a full-fledged social friendship in which you get together after work, go to social events together, share personal information, or meet extended family and friends. What you often begin with is a business friendship.

A business friendship should be a two-way street. You get and you also give. It may not be purely a one-for-one give-and-take in which you closely tally the score, but you do want to give back if you have gotten a benefit. This is part of friendship lite.

One of the surprises of friendship lite is how easy it can be to create this kind of relationship. It is not a deep or intense relationship. It is based on a comfortable interaction in which you help the other person to feel good about interacting with you. Friendship lite is a brief, positive interaction that has the potential for long-term growth.

The degree of continued social connection can also be affected by the status of the person you are interacting with. If you are connecting with a person who is older and more established, such as a boss or a judge, you are less likely to develop a social friendship out of the networking meeting. Think of the more senior people as the wizards. They have had the opportunity to develop deep connections in the community you are trying to join. You do want to try to meet with as many wizards as possible, because they are so knowledgeable about the market, the workplaces, the work-flow, and more. They may be friends of the gatekeepers and key keepers who are also from the same age group, having worked their way up in the ranks in their practice area. But the relationship will be affected by a person's status. A judge has to be mindful of any appearance of impropriety, for example. If your boss is significantly older, that generational difference might affect the degree of social interaction that evolves from your networking meeting. These and other social factors might influence the degree of social connection stemming from your networking.

However, when it comes to continuing a business friendship, age does not need to be a barrier. If you can help someone older than you or younger than you to be successful in a business context, you want to try to do so.

Why You Need to Give Back

The minute you pick up a phone to call a knight or wizard, you are starting a new relationship.

If you are concerned about bothering the person you are about to call, or you think that what you are doing is an imposition, you will probably never make the phone call at all. It is true that you are asking a stranger to give you time and advice. And if a total stranger called you and asked you to move furniture or paint a fence with him, you would probably not want to do that. But your request for advice and information is different.

First, you have vetted people to find the natural counselors. These are people who like to counsel and advise others. You can tell because you have used the voice test. What you are asking these people to do is something they enjoy. It is not as if you are asking a total stranger to move furniture with you or paint your fence. Your request is like asking a book lover to go to a book fair or a football fan to go to a game with you. The person enjoys the activity you are inviting him to do.

In addition, you have been introduced by a trusted contact. You are not a total stranger making a cold call. A mutual friend is the go-between. Because of that connection, you benefit from the extension of good will from one friend to another. You are getting the reflected positive feeling from that friendship. This is generally true even if your relationship with the trusted contact is only a limited level of interaction that is positive, friendship lite.

Having said that, meeting with you will take time. Knights and wizards are very busy people. In the context of the quest, these lawyers are racing around on their chargers, dashing through the forest on their way to business meetings, hearings, depositions, social events, and bar association lunches. If a knight or wizard spends time with you, you want to be sure she does not regret it.

How can you repay a knight or a wizard?

Good Deeds

You can give simple gifts to people who are good enough to spend time with you and help you. These gifts do not have to cost a lot. Some of them will only cost you time and effort.

There are gifts of attention, information, promotion, and connection, as well as inexpensive tangible gifts or thank-you notes.

A Gift of Attention. Listening, truly listening to someone else, is a gift. These days it is rare for a person to have uninterrupted time to talk, to express a concern, or to tell a story and have another person's undivided attention. It is rare for a person to get to talk without having the other person preach, dictate, or prescribe action. Having "air time" to convey thoughts and ideas, to speak openly and honestly, is rapidly becoming a casualty of modern day life for many people. We may be more plugged in to electronic devices such as cell phones and computers, but often that communication is more of a sound bite, a rapid exchange of information, a "tweet," not a leisurely conversation. Face-to-face interpersonal interaction is not as prevalent in general. Who is really listening to anyone these days?

Give your contact person the gift of being heard and supported.

Attentive listening means asking a question and letting the other person answer without interruption, asking follow-up questions to encourage more talking. It also means being supportive, empathic, and nonjudgmental, and having good eye contact and turning off the mobile devices.

Ask open-ended questions to be supportive:

"How long has this been going on?" "What have you done so far to try to help him?" "What resources have you looked into?"

Be empathic:

"That must be hard for you to deal with." "I'm sorry your Dad has developed cancer."

Be non-judgmental:

"How did your son get involved in this kind of problem? How is this affecting you?"

Not:

"You have to tell the authorities what he is doing. Why haven't you done that?"

It may be that the person you are talking with does not want to engage in this kind of conversation. That's fine. Never push it. But if your contact wants to discuss a problem at work or even a problem with a family member such as a son who has just had a DUI or a problem finding a nursing home for her father, you should encourage the discussion. The person may need the "air time."

Paying attention is a gift.

A Gift of Information. Providing another person with information can be a wonderful way to give back. The information a contact person needs could be work related or more personal in nature. For example, if you find out your contact has just lost a nanny and needs a replacement and you know of a good nanny service, that could be valuable information for your contact person. You could send an e-mail after your meeting to provide your contact with the website or phone number of the nanny agency you used to find a wonderful caretaker. If you can think of a good book, website, or blog to help your contact person to get needed useful information, you can provide that information. Books can be especially nice gifts. Write your thank-you note in the flyleaf:

> "Thank you for spending time with me last Friday. I really enjoyed meeting you and learning so much from you about litigation boutiques. Here is the book I mentioned at lunch about marketing for litigators. I hope you enjoy reading it."

Providing useful personal and professional information is a gift.

A Gift of Promotion. Most lawyers need to develop and maintain a positive image in their professional communities. Writing and speaking are two good ways to develop and maintain a presence. If you are in a position to help your contact person develop and maintain a professional presence, that is a gift.

If you co-chair a bar association committee, for example, and you are able to offer your contact person the opportunity to speak on a panel or at a lunch meeting, contribute to a webinar, contribute an article to a journal, or write a piece for your blog, that will help your contact person's professional career.

Giving your contact the opportunity for professional recognition is a gift.

A Gift of Connection. Professional careers thrive by meeting new people. If you know someone who would benefit by meeting this new contact person, help both people by connecting them. You can simply send an e-mail introduction to each person giving the background of each person to the other and why you think they ought to meet each other.

> "It was very helpful for me to spend time talking with you about corporations that you know about. I learned so much. After our meeting, I thought of a good person for you to meet. He is also in-house counsel at a midsize company and is facing some of the same challenges you mentioned at lunch. I am sending him an e-mail introducing you. I hope the two of you get together. I am certain you will enjoy meeting each other."

> "I have season tickets for the Cubs, and I would like to invite you and a friend of mine, who is also a great guy, to join me. The two of you should meet. You are both dealing with many of the same headaches. I know you like the Cubs, so let me know if you can do this and I'll set it up."

Connecting people who could benefit from knowing each other is a valuable gift.

A More Tangible Gift. Sometimes it makes sense to spend a few dollars to send a tangible gift to a contact person who has spent time with you and helped you. It could be a card with a handwritten note or something more.

One of my clients, a new graduate, had a very helpful networking lunch meeting with a woman who worked in-house as a health care lawyer. In the course of their conversation, they talked about recent vacations they had enjoyed. The health care lawyer had just returned from a trip to New Orleans where she had discovered jazz music. They connected around this topic. The new graduate had been a fan of jazz for many years. To thank her contact for spending time talking with her, she purchased a CD by one of her favorite jazz artists and sent it to the health care lawyer with a note thanking her for her time.

> "Thank you for spending time with me. I learned so much from you about the field of health care law. When I heard you say that you had discovered jazz, I thought you might enjoy this CD by a wonderful jazz artist who is one of my own favorites."

Tangible gifts should be small and based on a person's interests that you learn in your face-to-face meeting. Books are great gifts. If you learn that your contact enjoys mountain climbing, skiing, salsa dancing, travel, or is raising a child or training a dog or engaged in some other endeavor, buy a book that reflects that interest.

When to Thank Your Knights and Wizards More Formally

When you network for information and advice and develop lite friendships that have the potential to be more substantial friendships, there can be times when the lines of formality and informality blur. For example, you meet a knight to discuss what it is like to work at a smaller firm. In the process of that meeting, you learn that the firm is in need of a lawyer with your background, so you ask to be considered by the firm. That information changes the way you interact with the knight going forward. The relationship should become more formal. In this case, you would not send a handwritten note and small gift, because that would take on the appearance of impropriety. It might look as if you are trying to influence the person you've met to hire you by sending a present to him or her. If you are being considered for a job, every interaction should be formal and documented. Communications should be in writing. And gifts are not appropriate when you are being considered for a position.

9   Interviews

As you have been networking your way to job opportunities, you have already been engaging in interviews. In your encounters with knights and wizards, they have asked why you are leaving your firm, what you are looking for, and what you are trying to accomplish with your career. Each time a contact person asks you these questions, you have the opportunity to advocate for yourself and to use the opportunity to learn more about what is happening in your target market and at the specific firm where your contact person works. Whether or not these meetings are called interviews, they are interviews. They are discussions that could lead to a job.

There are three main types of interviews that occur in a job quest:

➤ Informational
➤ Informal
➤ Formal

Be prepared to advocate for yourself in an appropriate way for these interviews. Prepare anecdotal evidence. Prepare for the interview as if for an oral argument. Know your background. Know your value in the market. Understand how to create good "music" in your interview.

The Informational Interview

As you wend your way through the woods encountering the knights, wizards, and ogres and meeting with wizards and knights in person, the conversations you have with these contact people are often termed informational in nature. You are learning. You are interacting with these people to learn important information for your search. You need to hear about the lay of the land, and you also need to create relationships. Where is the work flowing? Who are the key players in the village? Which castles might have an interest in you given your background and your skill set? Who is the keeper of the castle keys?

As you gather this information, you are also creating new friendships, deepening existing friendships, and creating trust relationships. You are also actively engaged in helping the knights and wizards you meet by providing them with gifts of information, connection, promotion, and attention to help their work lives or lives outside of work to go better. By the time you have met with or at least talked with 20–40 of these contact people you could probably write an article for a magazine on this topic: where are there good opportunities for work for a person with your background and skills in this particular legal community? You are learning about the castles you think match up with your skill set and learning about the identity of the key keeper as well as hearing the gossip about these workplaces.

The informational interview can rapidly turn into an informal interview and, on occasion, can shift to a formal interview as well. This can happen if the knight or wizard meeting with you realizes that you could be an addition to his workplace. This can happen most readily if the wizard or knight you are meeting with is a gatekeeper or even the keeper of the castle keys. It can also happen if *you* realize you are a good match for this castle, and you suggest that you could be useful by saying the key words that shift the meeting from informational to informal interview:

> "I have no idea if your workplace would have an interest in someone with my background but would it make sense to start a conversation with whoever is in charge of hiring. By the way, who is that person?"

The Informal Interview

An informal interview is a meeting in which you are being vetted for a job but the setting is more casual, and the agenda may be lunch and a conversation. Sometimes, that lunch turns out to be an initial interview and the beginning of a vetting process for a job. The informal interview can happen during a job quest when the person meeting with you in an informal setting has an interest in vetting you for a possible job but does not tell you that up front. There can be many reasons for that lack of candor. The person meeting with you may not have the authority to hire, but only to suggest candidates. The person meeting with you may not be sure you will turn out to be a good prospect and needs to meet with you first to make that threshold determination.

If you have not met with the castle staff person—firm representative—yet, do not get your hopes up. The vetting partner or associate may not want the pressure of having to discuss job prospects in his castle. There may not be well-defined job prospects at his workplace. There may be no posting on the website or anywhere else. Until the vetting person meets you, there is no way to know if you are going to be the right lawyer to bring on board. As a result, sometimes there is a little dance that people do around the interview. It is termed an informal meeting or just lunch, when it can be more than that.

Another possibility is that the person meeting with you might initially believe she is just helping to inform you about the market, but by the time you are done with lunch, if you are impressive enough, she may be trying to figure out a way to bring you on board because you are just too outstanding to pass up.

From the job seeker's perspective, it doesn't matter whether the meeting with the contact person is billed as an informational or informal interview. The way to approach such a meeting is *as if* it is an interview. You want to be prepared to advocate for yourself and present strong answers to questions you are likely to be asked at any stage of the networking process.

Sometimes, a job will be created for a person who networks effectively into the hidden job market, makes a good impression, has the right core competencies for a workplace that is busy and growing, and is ready to advocate for himself in an informational or informal meeting.

The Formal Interview

The formal interview is the interview that people tend to think of as the "real" interview. This is supposed to be the one that counts. And for some castles, that may be the case. If you apply for a position using more formal channels, as you must with a large firm or company, if you use a recruiter, or you apply for a government job through usajobs.gov, the federal jobs website, or via a website posting for a company, you will, hopefully, land a formal interview. However, as we already know, when you apply online or to a website posting, or use a recruiter, you have to get past the dragon at the drawbridge to get to a formal interview. Depending on the workplace, an informational or informal interview that brings you to the attention of those in charge of hiring might be every bit as important as the formal interview, because these are the vetting exercises that get you to the next level of scrutiny.

At times, in fact, the formal interview may be pro forma. This can happen when you make it through the informal meetings where the tough questions are asked and answered well. By the time you reach the formal interview stage the only real question left might be whether you fit into the workplace culture (Do they like you?) and how much you will cost the workplace if you are hired. You have already been vetted by key people for your skill set and passed that test.

In short, it is important to be prepared for a good interview as soon as you set foot outside the cottage and begin your quest.

Be Ready for the Interview from the Start of Your Quest

The difference in the preparation for informational, informal, and formal interviews is simple: there is none. Once the rest of the equation is met—the work is there, your skills match or are close enough, and you have a trusted contact or credible endorsements—it comes down to good energy or interactions that are comfortable, and how much you will cost if you are hired.

You need to be ready for the formal interview as soon as you start your quest, before you meet your first knight or wizard, because you do not know when an informational interview could turn into an informal interview or even a formal interview. The casual meeting can shift to a probe of your skill set, background, and legal knowledge whether you indicate your job interest or not.

The Importance of Anecdotal Evidence to Persuade

The interview is your opportunity to advocate for yourself. Just as the networking phase is about friendship, the interview phase is about advocacy.

It is an opportunity to help the potential employer to understand how you could be a valuable addition to the castle. It is an opportunity to help the potential employer to feel reassured that you are a good choice for the job. To prepare for an interview, think about the potential employer's needs. Ask yourself what you would want to see in a candidate's skill set and background if you were the employer. If you can figure out the employer's needs, you can prepare for your interview more effectively. Check the company or firm website. Try to read articles about this work- place. Talk with people who once worked there, especially if they worked there recently. You can sometimes find these people using LinkedIn or an old and a new directory of lawyers in the city where the firm is located. Talk with people who work at comparable places where the skill set is likely to be similar.

Just as you may be nervous about landing a job with this employer, potential employers are also nervous. Unless they have worked with you before, they have to develop some degree of confidence that you can and will be the right person for the job. What if you turn out not to be the kind of employee you say you are? Anticipating the concerns of potential employers is important. They need to be reassured that you will be a good hire.

You accomplish this by producing solid evidence, as good trial lawyers do. When it comes to the interview, your evidence is anecdotal. Amazingly, many lawyers who would never think to try a case without marshalling their physical evidence go into interviews without preparing strong anecdotal evidence to convince this tribunal of potential employers.

When I ask most lawyers, "Why would you be a good hire for this position?" a typical answer usually sounds something like, "I am a hard worker and I always give every job I do 110 percent," "I am bright and capable and intelligent," or "I am very responsible."

These answers are conclusions. They are general statements. But they are not good advocacy. What if a lawyer were to say to a jury or a judge, "I think you should side with me because the defendant is really guilty." That is unconvincing. It does not answer the question, "Why should we believe what you said? How do we know this is true? What is the evidence?" If you can only come up with conclusions, you will not have a convincing case.

The way you marshal your evidence for the interview is in the form of anecdotal material. If you hear yourself saying something that is a conclusionary statement, such as "I am a hard worker," then you need to force yourself to supplement your answer with supportive anecdotal documentation, such as the following.

> "I have a long history of being a hard worker. When I wrote for the *Michigan Law Review*, I not only edited my own pieces, but I routinely stayed until 2:00 A.M. the night before submission to the printer to review all of the articles for typos or errors. I am still the same today. Just last week we had an emergency motion, and I was the one who stayed overnight to be sure everything was done perfectly before we filed the next day. I don't mind doing that. I truly love doing this kind of work, and it's important to me that the work be done at the highest level."

> "I am a good lawyer. I say that because I work really hard, and I have a good ability to understand legal concepts. For example, when our office got a case involving a Mafia figure who used an offshore bank to hide his assets, I realized fairly quickly that we could urge the court to support a new application of an old precedent, which would then allow the FBI access to certain bank documents that had been excluded from discovery until this point. We prevailed using that new theory. I thoroughly enjoyed writing the brief that changed the law in this area."

Remember that the anecdotal material must be honest. No exaggeration allowed. If you have done a good job in the past, there should be no need to pretend to be anything more than you are. In fact you want to assert the truth about your level of performance and skills, because if you land the job, you will be expected to perform at that level. If you disappoint your employer, that could mean poor reviews and even eventual job loss.

Be aware that in the interview you can talk about what other people have said about you. It is hearsay and it might be objectionable in court, but it is perfectly fine in an interview. If your partner or a client has said great things about you, you can quote them in your interview. It may sound less self-congratulatory to have a third-party comment about you than for you to praise yourself. It is more credible to the listener to hear, "After we finished the trial, the client wrote a letter to my partner saying he had never seen a more dedicated, bright associate and asked to have me included on the trial team in any future matters."

What other anecdotal information should you prepare for your interview? As you think about what a potential employer would want from a person doing the job you are hoping to do, identify the key elements you would look for from that worker. Here is a partial list of typical traits and skills that legal employers like to know you possess:

1. Loyalty
2. Energy
3. Perseverance
4. Attention to detail
5. Honesty and truthfulness
6. Ethical standards
7. Ability to research, write, and understand legal concepts
8. Street smarts
9. People skills
10. Ability to work on a team
11. Ability to follow directions
12. Ability to work for long hours without complaint
13. Likeability
14. Real enjoyment of the practice of law
15. Good judgment

For every one of these traits, you should prepare short stories from your past that illustrate that you possess these traits.

One great way to find out the list of traits that an employer would like you to have is by having an informational interview with someone in a comparable job. By doing that you will find out what the person believes one needs to be successful in a position that is similar. Take notes. Then prepare your list of traits to prove up using your background as evidence.

Another way to discover this list of traits and skills is to find an advertisement for a comparable job and see what the job requirements are, write out the list, and identify the evidence that you can point to in your experience for each trait or skill. Just keep in mind that ads and web-site postings will not mention the personal, intangible characteristics that may be important factors for landing the job: factors such as an ability to get along with other people on the team, maintain a good disposition, or work well with a micromanaging boss. Yet, they may be the most impor-tant traits for landing the job.

You can address these unstated material requirements by anticipat-ing that your personal qualities matter to the interviewer. You can give examples and illustrations of how you work well on a team, maintain a good attitude under pressure, or work well with difficult and demanding partners by using anecdotal material that establishes those points in your interview.

How do you know if the workplace is interested in certain personal qualities, and how do you know which ones matter? If you have networked your way to the key keeper, you have already been hearing about the workplace. You have heard about people in the hierarchy and the culture of the workplace, the gossip about the workplace, and the good and bad news about some of the people who work there. Networking is the best way to learn about these intangibles that can be extremely helpful to you when you prepare your case to be hired.

Why a Good Interview Is Like an Oral Argument

In a typical interview, you will be asked questions that you will need to answer, but you also have a core agenda that you want to advance. While you are answering questions, you are also trying to work in your key points. In an oral argument before a panel of judges, you have the same situation. The judges fire questions at you and you answer them, but you also need to get across those key points that shape the way the judges view the facts of your case and the legal precedents that influence their decisions.

Your core agenda in the interview is to answer the question, "Why should we hire you over the competition?" If you can answer that question by identifying the reasons you will be a great choice for this job, you have the basis for the advocacy argument that you need to make in your interview. Write out the answer before you go to any interview or before you call the gatekeeper or the knight who could help you get a formal interview with the key keeper.

It is not always possible to get your entire advocacy message out in response to one question, but you want to be determined to get it all out there at some point before you shake hands and say goodbye. Keep your key points in mind. As you make your points in the interview, you can check them off your mental list of things to be sure to say. Of course, you want to repeat them in your thank-you letter.

Know Your Background

It is a given that you should be knowledgeable about your own background and skills. But it is also crucial to be knowledgeable about the law in your practice area particularly as it relates to any of your past cases. Thus, in addition to the dates and chronology of your work history, you also need to be able to speak comfortably about every case and concept you allude to in your résumé. You need to be ready to answer the question "What was the most difficult case you have dealt with?" with a clear understanding of the facts and legal concepts attendant to the case as well as what ultimately happened. The more proficient you are about talking about legal concepts with ease and accuracy, the more impressive you will be to the interviewer, and the more likely that the key keeper will want to hire you to work at the castle.

Know Your Value in the Marketplace

Once you have convinced the key keeper that your skills are right and that you will fit in, the issue of compensation will need to be addressed. You have to know your value in the marketplace and your value to this castle specifically.

Learning compensation levels is easier if the workplace is one that is well known to recruiters, is a larger organization that participates in the *American Lawyer Magazine* pay scale questionnaire, participates in a survey for the National Association for Law Placement, or is a governmental entity. A boutique firm or smaller workplace will not be as likely to have published pay scales. The way to find out what lawyers make at these workplaces is to conduct a few informational phone calls or e-mails to ask friends at comparable firms or organizations what the acceptable pay range might be. Never ask what your friend actually makes.

The compensation dance can be a tricky one. Try not to discuss compensation too early in the vetting process if you can avoid it. The discussion of compensation is best left for later meetings. You want the employer to really want to hire you before you address the issue. If you are asked what you want to make early in the vetting process and you answer but are too high compared to others with comparable skills or too high compared to what the workplace is ready to pay, then you can be summarily removed from the interview process and lose your chance to advocate for yourself. If you happen to come in too low, you might be considered a less stellar lawyer, or you might be hired as a bargain but feel cheated and disappointed when you learn what you make compared to others in comparable jobs at the same or similar castles. One way to postpone an early discussion is to say, "I care a great deal about the work I will be doing and the people I will be working with. If you believe I am right for the job and I want to work here, then I am absolutely certain that we will come to a meeting of the minds about the level of compensation. But I think we still have to discuss some things first before we get to that question."

What could make this topic trickier are economic concerns. You may not want to ruin your chance for a job by playing hardball in a recession. So when you attempt to postpone this discussion, watch the interviewer's reaction. If you sense that you are disappointing the interviewer, and if you are concerned that you will be throwing away a job you really want, try a different tactic. Say, "I would be interested to know more about how this firm handles compensation, and I would like to learn whatever the current compensation level is for people with my background. What would that be?" Be open to the needs of the workplace, but also know your personal limitations and your bottom-line salary requirements.

There are also situations that require that you name your compensation level early in the process. For example, if you are working with a recruiter, it will waste everyone's time if you are not able to identify your salary range. Give the range you want but add that what matters most is the job and people you will be working with. Salary requirements do not need to be a deal breaker if the job is right in other ways.

If you answer an ad and it requires that you state your salary requirements, you may have to do so to get to the next level of scrutiny. This is another reason why online ads have limitations for job seekers—it may be impossible to respond with full or nuanced answers.

Understand How to Create Good Music in the Interview

The question of whether you will fit into the culture of the workplace is the "music" between you and the castle staff that is vetting you for a job. This is not just the schools you attended or your clerkship, but how comfortable it is to talk with you. Do you have shared interests with the interviewer or with potential coworkers? Are you pleasant to have around whether or not you have much in common with others? This can come down to personalities clicking, and it is something that you do not have much control over. It is generally not even directly mentioned in the interview. No one is going to say something awkward such as: "Will we like working with you? Are you someone who will work well with our team?", but you can be certain that is what your interviewers are wondering when they conduct the interview. Typically, a key keeper and others involved in the interview process assess that "fit" factor by seeing how you act in the interview.

If you get terribly nervous in an interview, you might say something that is disarmingly honest such as, "You know I really am excited about this job, and I feel pretty nervous right now about this interview because I would really like to work here." That might help the interviewer to feel good about you even if you seem uptight.

Sometimes it helps to imagine that the interview is taking place in your home and you are the one welcoming the interviewer into the place where you live. Pretend you are having a party and the interviewer is your guest. You want the interviewer to feel welcome. Instead of thinking about how nervous you feel in your interview, this device might help you to adopt a frame of mind in which you are helping the interviewer to feel more at ease.

Making a good connection in the interview is one of the single most important intangible aspects of your quest. That is one reason why it is usually a good idea to include interesting hobbies and community activities on your résumé. Sometimes a shared hobby is the key to having a lot of fun in your interview and helps you to land the job you have worked so hard to find.

Manage Tough Questions

When you are on a job quest, you meet many people you have never met before, and they may ask why you are searching for a job. If you have been fired, that might be a question you would prefer not to answer. In truth, what you fear may be embarrassment. Most attorneys are high-performing type-A people, who have had many successes in life and will have many more in the future. Being let go may be the first disappointing event of your career. It is normal to be worried about talking with people who will ask why you are leaving your job. Should you tell the truth and say, "I was fired," or should you try to pretend it did not happen? Some attorneys who have been fired are so unnerved by the experience that they avoid networking in person to circumvent uncomfortable questions that could lead to an admission about being let go. When faced with a direct question about outplacement, some attorneys lie about it and say they were not fired. This is not the best approach. Castle staff, gatekeepers, and key keepers at the castle where you are interviewing might have back-channel conversations with villagers, castle staff, gatekeepers, and key keepers in other castles in which they might learn about the truth of your situation. If that happens, your candidacy is more likely to be in jeopardy than if you had told the truth from the beginning. If you have been fired or outplaced by your firm, you have to be ready to handle questions about that. It is understandable to want to avoid uncomfortable conversations about what could be perceived as your failure, either by pretending you were not let go or by sending your résumé to the castle directly and bypassing all face-to-face contact. Remember that the uncomfortable questions are going to come up eventually, not just from friends, family, and others who are trying to help you, but also from gatekeepers, knights, wizards, and the key keeper when you meet for an interview. You must prepare for that and any other dreaded questions. You want to have a consistent statement that you tell people so that you are not tripped up by back-channel conversations about your reason for embarking on this quest.

It is usually best to address the issue realistically and without pretense. Deal with uncomfortable questions by planning what you will say and practice with friends and family. If you have been let go, your attitude about that event is probably the most important part of your answer. If you convey confidence that you will find another good opportunity, that you have learned from this experience, and that you see this outplacement or termination as a positive career move that could result in something better, that positive attitude will have a good effect on the interviewer.

In a recession especially, there is no reason to define an outplacement as a personal failure. Many law firms experience a significant reduction in the amount of legal matters they work on when the economy is not growing. Decisions made by managing partners at the firm about which lawyers to let go will often be dictated by a perceived overabundance of lawyers at a certain level of practice or a need for a practice group to cut back generally because there is a lack of work in that particular practice area. Decisions to fire workers during difficult economic times are often made with great reluctance since the firm has invested time, money, and effort recruiting and training these lawyers. Your firm's lack of work was not the result of your job performance. In a robust economy, the same lawyers would not have been let go. There is no reason to feel ashamed.

Simply explain that you are one of many lawyers leaving the firm as part of an economic shift that many firms and companies have experienced lately.

"I'm one of ten associates and partners who has been let go by the firm. Our firm has been deeply affected by the current economy. The firm had to downsize."

Or say:

"This is an economic outplacement. I was assured of that by the partner I work with most closely. I want you to call him so that you can be sure of that."

My clients are often surprised to discover that when they talk honestly with people who can advance their job quests, they receive great support and warmth from those they open up to. If job seekers can admit that they were fired or outplaced, many receive greater encouragement and assistance from the people they encounter. Some are genuinely surprised by the degree of empathy and engagement they experience when they confide in total strangers as they network for new opportunities.

Stay on the Radar

Once you have found a prospective castle or cottage, try to stay in touch with someone inside. You can connect with your contact person who may be a wizard, a knight, a gatekeeper for the castle, castle staff or the keeper of the keys. You can stay in touch with your contact person by e-mail and express your continued interest. Have coffee with your contact every so often. Do good deeds when you can using your intuitive judgment about the extent of your gifts of connection, promotion, listening, and information. The idea is to stay on the castle's radar as a person who is likeable and has a skill set that is valuable to the castle so that if and when they develop a need, they are thinking about you to fill it.

Throughout the interview process, remain vigilant. If you do not know much about a given castle because you have not done much research on it, you may be concerned that it is not what you are looking for. Keep in mind that if it is the wrong castle, you will be able to figure this out by checking it against your Essential Elements. By using your Essential Elements template to measure the workplace for your personal needs, you are vetting the castle for your unique requirements. Even if you have questions about the castle or are not sure the castle needs help yet, go through with the interview, because it could turn out that you are at the right place at the right time. You might be "getting lucky."

10 The Treasure Chest Concept

You are finding your way through the forest, talking with people, learning from them and meeting new people with their assistance. You are figuring out how to get to the right castles. In the process you are already having interviews. As you conduct your quest, you want to be open, take risks, and be fearless about talking with many knights and wizards. Occasionally you may encounter a knight or wizard who is a virtual treasure, because he or she links you to the person you hoped to meet, or is actually the very gatekeeper or key keeper you were hoping to connect with. This is the Treasure Chest concept. In this chapter you will learn how it works to further your quest.

What Is the Treasure Chest Concept?

Every so often a hidden treasure chest is discovered somewhere in the world. It might be on the bottom of the sea near a wrecked Spanish galleon or on a deserted island that pirates frequented. Someone finds a treasure chest. No one knows what is inside. There could be Spanish doubloons, golden goblets or coins in the box. On the other hand, there might be nothing but dirt and sand in there. The only way to find out what is inside is to open it up.

People can be treasure chests too; Their treasure is crucial information or other assistance for your quest. Every person you meet is an unopened box of possibility, a potential treasure chest. You do not know what vital information a person holds unless and until you "open the treasure chest." How do you do that?

Think: You Never Know . . .

The *treasure chest concept* resulted from my observations of job seekers over many years. Some job seekers had preconceived expectations about who would be helpful to them and who would not. Many networkers thought this way:

> "If the person I am going to contact does not have a clear connection to a possible job, then it's not worth my time to try to meet up."

The default position for many networkers seemed to be a belief that a contact person must be directly linked to a potential job to be worth the effort to connect and meet in person.

I also observed that many of the lucky networkers were finding out that contact people they did not expect to be very helpful were in fact giving them important leads and good information and sometimes were even joining their round table and contributing advice and guidance. Often the first person in a line of linked contacts would not provide the job search treasure, but if the networker persevered and continued to network from contact to contact to contact, going beyond their closer friends into the realm of strangers, they would eventually hear of the opportunity that would provide that one great job they needed.

This makes sense when you realize that every person you know knows at least 100 other people, if not more. When you first start your quest, you are tapping into another person's knowledge and contact base, but that person does not have contacts that reach into every corner of the neighborhood. People are most familiar with their own small part of that larger neighborhood you are entering. Most people do not know about activity across the entire neighborhood unless it is a very small community. For this reason, you need to move further into the neighborhood you are targeting and tap into other subgroups of connections to gain knowledge. As you progress, you get a fuller picture of your targeted legal neighborhood. You learn more about key people and which workplaces are busy and have good reputations.

You may also find people who will link you to the very gatekeepers or key keepers you were trying to connect with. Sometimes, the person you are talking to turns out to be the very gatekeeper or key keeper you were trying to locate, or you may discover a new friend who is able to connect you immediately to the gatekeeper, key keeper or castle that is the goal of your quest. If that happens you have discovered treasure.

Open Up the Box by Discovering Connections

Networkers who push beyond their close friends, into the realm of the knights and wizards—those strangers who are natural counselors and willing to be helpful—frequently report surprising coincidences such as the discovery of common friends and similar strong interests with these new contacts. They are delighted to learn that they or their close family members have attended the same schools or colleges, or lived in the same cities or neighborhoods at one time in their lives, and may have enjoyed going to the same restaurants or have had similar experiences growing up, like the same music, share the same politics, have children with similar issues, and much more. These discovered connections are not only fun, they are also wonderfully helpful. Both the job seeker and newly discovered friend often feel closer as a result of finding a surprising connection or commonality. That new friend is usually more engaged and invested in the job seeker's quest in ways that would not have happened without that sense of affiliation and connectivity.

Job seekers usually attribute these surprising connections to luck, but once you are aware of the treasure chest concept and consciously apply it, it can be a valuable networking tool. These discovered connections are common and remarkably helpful for any job seeker. Every job seeker needs to try to uncover their shared interpersonal connections with other people because it helps to create greater affiliation, attachment, and engagement. But the connection to the other person needs to be genuine and mutual, not merely self-serving. People are good judges of credibility. People know when you are sincerely interested in creating a friendship or out for your own personal gain.

Open Up the Box by Talking About Your Dream and Dilemma

When you meet with people who are in a position to directly help you fulfill your job quest, you want to be sure you give them the right information and the best guidance you can so that they can maximize their ability to assist you. You have done a great deal of work to prepare for this and other meetings with knights and wizards. You have figured out what you want in a job, the type of place you would like to work, studied where the work-flow seems to be, and begun to learn about the castles and the people in the neighborhood that you hope to join and you have prepared for your interview. When you happen upon a person who yields a treasure, you want to be ready to guide him or her to advance your quest. You must also be ready to advocate for yourself. Part of that advocacy is revealing your dream and your dilemma to this well-positioned person.

Why is it important to use the words dream and dilemma? Because when you tell helpful people your dream and your problem fulfilling it, it motivates people to help you. When you share that information with others who are primed to help you, they care more and do more to assist your job search. If using the words *dream* or *dilemma* sounds too corny or dramatic, then use the words *goal* and *problem*, or *objective* and *difficulty*. Any of these pairings is effective.

When you share your dream, goal, or objective, and you use clear prototypes and enough detail to create an image for them, you help your contact not only identify places and people who could advance your search, but identify personally with your vision. If you say you have a dream of becoming the best litigator you can be or you have the goal of learning everything you can about health care law, or you want to be able to handle complex real estate transactions, you are revealing your aspirations. You have already vetted this person and determined that he or she is a knight or wizard, someone who likes to help others if you have used the voice test. When you create an image of your aspirations, a knight, wizard or gatekeeper is likely to join you and try to assist you. The Make-a-Wish Foundation works on this principle. People who like to help others like to help others realize their dreams, goals, or objectives. It feels good. It is empathically gratifying. But it only feels good if they also like you and have a sense of connection with you.

When you share your dilemma, you are revealing the barrier to your success. If you say, for example,

> "I am hoping to become the best trial lawyer I can be and find opportunities at really outstanding litigation boutiques, but I don't know anyone who is presently working at a place like that; I am not sure how to connect with that group of lawyers. Do you?"

you are presenting your contact person with an opportunity to do something concrete to help you to achieve your dream, vision, goal. You have chosen to talk with this person because you have some reason to believe he or she does know that group of lawyers you are trying to meet and will be able to connect you with at least a few of them. You have now given this person the way to assist you. You are giving a person who likes to help others solve problems a chance to help you solve your problem.

If you have the good fortune to be talking with a gatekeeper or a key keeper, you should ask for an interview. If you tell this person that your goal is to work in his castle and tell him why this is your goal, it shows your contact that you believe this workplace is the best fit for you. It is also a compelling reason to give you a shot at a job, especially if you are an appropriate candidate who has done your homework and knows the competition but chooses this workplace. You don't want just any job. You would really like this specific job at this specific place.

The Treasure Chest Concept in Action

A good illustration of the treasure chest concept comes from my own experience after graduating from law school. As I mentioned earlier in the book, I had gone to law school with the intention of becoming a prosecutor after graduation. My plan was to work as an assistant district attorney in Philadelphia. I sent my résumé to that office, but I did not receive a response. Since some of my friends were getting hired by the D.A.'s office, I asked them what they had done to get an interview. My friends told me that without a personal connection to the current office, I did not have a very good chance of getting an interview, let alone a job.

I tried to think of anyone I knew who was even tangentially connected with the current district attorney's office. I thought of a friend I had worked with at a social service agency before going to law school, because I had heard that her husband was a lawyer and was politically active in the current administration. I had met my friend's husband only briefly. When I met him, however, I thought he was a pretty serious guy, tight-lipped at first, but with interesting ideas that came out once he began talking. I had no idea what his job was in the administration.

I would have reconnected with my friend under any circumstances since I was genuinely interested in getting to know both her and her husband better. But I also hoped to kick-start my networking by connecting with someone who was likely to know people in the district attorney's office. My hope was that my friend's husband would help me find the next person to talk with.

I called my friend and invited her and her husband to join me and my husband for dinner. I also mentioned that I would like to talk with her husband about what he knew about government jobs in Philadelphia. She was very open to that idea and said her husband would be happy to help me.

They accepted my invitation and when they came for dinner I made a point of renewing our friendship. We had a wonderful time. They talked about their children and told funny stories about their house renovation, which my husband and I were able to match with stories about the killer bees that took up residence in our backyard. We shared vacation stories and generally enjoyed the evening together. Finally we got to dessert. I gathered my courage and said to my friend's husband, "Before you go, John, I have to ask you about something. To put it bluntly, I have a dream and a dilemma. My dream is that I want to be a prosecutor and my dilemma is that I have no personal connection to the district attorney's office and I hear I am not getting in there without one. Do you have any advice for me?" To which he replied, "You do have a personal connection to that office. I'm the first assistant district attorney and our office is looking for more women to hire."

After I recovered from the surprise at hearing that news, I asked him if he would be willing to interview me. And he said he'd be very willing to do that. He just wanted to be certain that I truly wanted to be a prosecutor not a public defender, and I assured him of that. My interview took place over the next twenty minutes. I explained why I wanted to be a prosecutor and why I would do a good job. At the time, there was a primary election coming up for the position of district attorney. Emmett Fitzpatrick was the Democratic incumbent and current district attorney, but there was a chance he would not prevail in the primary against Ed Rendell. My friend's husband suggested that we see how the election turned out. If

Fitzpatrick won, he would set me up with an interview and said he would recommend me for the job.

I learned a lot from this experience. One thing I learned was to do my homework better. In the course of conducting my job quest, I made the mistake of failing to do thorough due diligence. I had the preconceived idea that I would only learn about the next person to network with, not dine with the guy in charge of hiring. Even though I made a mistake in thinking that way, I also did something right: I pursued the connection even though I did not expect it would be a direct link. If my friend's husband had turned out to have no connection with the district attorney's office, I was fully prepared to network from him to anyone he could introduce me to so that I could find my way to a gatekeeper for that office and try to have an interview. If he had not been able to help me, I would have pursued other leads. I was determined to make that luck happen.

The fact that this experience embodied a key concept for networking did not occur to me until I became a career counselor. For many years I thought I was just very lucky that my friend's husband turned out to be the first assistant district attorney. Over time, however, I saw this sort of scenario replicated with clients so often that I recognized a pattern. Job search luck improves if you take the approach that you cannot predict the outcome of a networking connection and you are willing to explore and invest in new relationships with an open mind.

As you conduct your quest never assume that you know the extent of a contact's knowledge or their contacts. Take the attitude that you never know what the next person you meet could help you to accomplish; you never know who the next person you meet could help you to meet. When you discover new people, explore the curious and sometimes surprising affiliations that can bring you closer to people you thought were unconnected strangers. What you will learn is that these new people have many things in common with you that bring you closer. The discovery of new friends enriches your job search and your life in ways that are unpredictable but often remarkably helpful.

Find job search treasure by exploring these commonalities and creating trust relationships that are authentic and mutual. Open the treasure chest by telling people your dream, goal or objective and your dilemma, problem, or difficulty.

Every person you meet on your quest could yield a hidden treasure.

11 Creative Networking

There are times during your quest when the treasure is not hidden. The person you really need to connect with is known to you or becomes known to you through your networking efforts, but you do not know how to meet up with that person. This is when you might decide to use creative networking to achieve key meetings with certain knights and wizards. You create an opportunity to meet with the person you need to connect with. You do this by using humor and being inventive, but never aggressive or pesky. You always try to come to the attention of the gatekeeper or key keeper through a trusted contact of that person.

What Is Creative Networking?

There are times when it makes sense to try to create an opportunity to meet with someone who could help you have a successful search. This has to be done only in appropriate circumstances; those circumstances will depend on the particular situation. Creative networking involves trying to meet with a key person you have no direct connection with, but whom you know could be helpful to you if you could get what amounts to an informal interview during which you can advocate for yourself.

When Do You Try It?

Before you try creative networking, be sure you fit the profile of the kind of person this workplace would be likely to hire. Go back to the rule governing who gets jobs. Jobs go to people with

1. the right background and skill set for the work being done at this workplace.
2. who come to the attention of this workplace through a trusted contact, with an endorsement, if possible.
3. where the workplace is busy and growing.
4. where the music is likely to be good between the job seeker and the interviewer(s).

The creative meet-up has to do with item #2, finding the trusted contact. Sometimes you create the trusted contact by networking in person and having good interviews and informal meetings with people who link you to the next contacts that get you closer to the castle's key keeper. Sometimes you can create the link by being inventive. Your intuitive judgment is important here, however. If you wonder whether your action might be misconstrued, check out your idea with friends and family or professors or colleagues who have good judgment and a willingness to be a sounding board for you. Your group of round-table knights could be a resource for you as you try to figure out if your plan for creative networking is going to be well received or not.

Networking Through Golf and a Helpful Wizard

One of my clients, a litigation partner at a midsized firm, wanted to move to Florida to be closer to his wife's family after the births of their children. He wanted to change his career direction also. He no longer wanted to be a lawyer. He wanted to move into a business role. He hoped to obtain an administrative position at a bank or hospital, but he had no direct experience in either realm. The only thing he had managed in his career was litigation.

He began his search for a job by contacting recruiters, but they were not responsive to his inquiries because he was trying to alter the kind of work he would be doing, so he did not fit within the parameters of the searches most executive or legal recruiters handle. Recruiters he spoke with suggested that he not try for too much, that he should move to Florida but continue to be a litigator. But when he tried to contact law firms in Florida, they wanted to know if he had portable practice (business he could bring with him), which he did not have. He tried sending résumés and cover letters to companies he thought might be interested in him, making the case that his litigation background had enhanced his management skills and prepared him for a management position at a hospital or bank. He had no luck with that approach either. Some of the companies to which he sent résumés and cover letters responded summarily with rejections, saying that they were not hiring.

When we began working together he was discouraged about his prospects for making this move. I also wondered if he was trying for too much. Moving to a new city and finding a job doing the same kind of work can be challenging enough. Relocating and changing career direction might be too hard to accomplish. Nonetheless, I gave him the job search training session, and then we brainstormed together. Did he have any gatekeepers, key keepers, or wizards who might help him out? Did he know anyone who might help him meet with this group of people in the location in Florida he was trying to move to?

After some thought, he told me he probably had a pretty good wizard. His father-in-law had been the head of a small company in the Florida town where he and his wife hoped to move. Although the father-in-law's business was not very large, it was successful and well run. His father-in-law had made many friends in the business community, especially with people in the banking industry. He was a joiner. He had been a pillar of the business community in that town, contributing to local causes and supporting charitable events. He was well liked. He had recently retired but still knew many people in that town. He was also eager to have his daughter and grandchildren move to Florida and live nearby.

So we put together a plan for my client to spend two long weekends in Florida playing golf. He contacted his father-in-law and asked him to set up a series of golf outings with people who were part of the hierarchy at some of the good local banks and who might be interested in talking with him if he came to their attention through a trusted contact, namely, his father-in-law. They agreed that if nothing developed from their networking efforts, at least they would have some fun on the golf course together.

The next time I met with my client was after the arranged golf outings. He was meeting with me to do a mock interview session in preparation for a series of interviews for a management position with one of the banks he had been hoping would vet him for a job. The golf outings had done the trick. He landed interviews at some of the very banks that had originally sent him letters telling him that they were not hiring. He was able to accomplish the move to Florida and shift his career at the same time.

The relationship with his father-in-law helped him to meet the key keepers and gatekeepers at some local banks. His interview helped him to seal the deal. Could he have accomplished the same result without his father-in-law's help? He might have found friends or past colleagues who were living in Florida or who knew people in Florida in the banking world. He might have moved to Florida, found an "of counsel" role at a litigation firm by networking, developed relationships with the people in banks that he hoped would eventually consider him for a management job, created a positive buzz for himself in the local community, and moved from there into the banking world on the business side. He might have networked into an in-house position as a lawyer at a smaller bank and moved from there to the business side of the bank. All of this is speculation, but it is not fantasy —this is the way many people develop their careers. It can take time and effort, but it can happen with good networking. In short, good networking can include crafting meetings with key people who then help you advance your search. Ideally, you work with people who know and like you already to locate those people who could advance your cause and move you closer to the hierarchy of the castles you would like to connect with. My client tapped into his father-in-law's network to set up informal meetings that moved him closer to the formal vetting process.

Going to the Dogs

One of my clients came to work with me to determine her career direction after leaving an in-house position. After doing the preliminary work to identify a good career direction, it was clear that she was a natural for management consulting for law firms. She was also a naturally good networker, and once she figured out the right career direction, she began the quest for information about where there might be a job in that very limited field in the city where she lived. She learned about a consulting job at a well-respected management consulting firm that had been vacated for a number of months. Through networking efforts, my client was able to confirm that the job had not been filled. She set about trying to find a way to get vetted for that position by coming to the attention of the workplace through a trusted contact.

My client knew of only one person in the field of management consulting for law firms and, as luck would have it, he lived right down the street from her. She did not know him personally, but she knew what he looked like, that he had a dog, and that he walked his dog at the same neighborhood dog park that she and her dog frequented. One day, when she saw her management consultant neighbor walking his dog past her home heading for the dog park, she quickly got her dog on a leash and set off after him.

Once at the park it was easy to meet him and start a conversation that led to a longer discussion. Through him, she learned about the management consulting firms in town and was able to obtain information about the company with the vacancy. She contacted the consulting firm and confirmed that the spot was unfilled. After that, she launched an effective campaign to convince this management consulting firm to hire her for that open position, which they eventually did.

Finding creative ways to meet up with important gatekeepers can be a useful strategy, but it has to be done in a reasonable way. You need to keep your efforts to connect with people within acceptable, conventional bounds based on the particular workplace culture and the particular situation. That means that you need to ask the knights and wizards you talk with about how that workplace tends to find their hires. Do they use recruiters? Do they rely on ads? Would you be welcome if you showed up in person on the doorstep? Sometimes you have to rely on your intuitive judgment and be sensitive to the circumstances. My client who found a creative way to "bump into" the management consultant at the dog park did it in a clever and effective way. Appearing at this man's home or at the consulting firm without any introduction would have been too unconventional to be seen in a positive light. She also impressed this consultant enough to meet with her more extensively.

A Tale of Two Creative Networking Attempts

Sometimes, despite your best effort to create a meeting, it does not have the desired result. One woman I worked with many years ago went to a fundraiser for the incumbent state's attorney hoping to meet with him there and express her interest in working at that office. There were many other people at the fundraiser that night, and presumably some of these people held more interest for the incumbent. She might have done better to volunteer at that state's attorney's office or land an externship and do outstanding work that would gain her recognition with people in the office who would then endorse her for a job as an assistant state's attorney.

She might have had a different experience at the fundraiser if she had networked more and found an endorser who also could connect her to either the state's attorney himself or to someone known and trusted by him. If that person had introduced her to the incumbent, she might have had better luck.

On the other hand, another client created her own luck at a fundraiser by finding a way to meet with the partner of a law firm she had hoped would interview her. She had seen the partner's name as a speaker at a fundraiser for a cause she had long been involved with, so she made sure to attend. After he spoke, she introduced herself and talked with him about their shared interest in this not-for-profit. Then she expressed her honest, long-standing interest in his firm. He asked her to come by for an interview, and although it took a few months for the firm to develop a need for a new hire at her level, she was hired by the firm about six months later.

A Creative Way to Meet Up with a Key Keeper

Another example of creating a meet-up comes from my own background. As I mentioned before in the section on the treasure chest concept, when I graduated from law school I applied to the district attorney's office in Philadelphia. I had been a social worker before going to law school, but I went to law school expressly to become a prosecutor. It was my dream job. So, after applying to the D.A.'s office, I waited, and heard nothing. Meanwhile, some of my friends from law school not only obtained interviews but job offers. After talking with my friends about how they were able to get interviews I learned that people who got hired by that office had connections. I did not have any connections.

I was incredibly discouraged. But understanding the reality also put me in a frame of mind that can best be described as willing to act creatively. If I had no chance to land the job of my dreams, then I had nothing to lose by pursuing it in an unorthodox way. At the time there was a primary campaign going on and the district attorney job was the subject of an intensely competitive race. The Democratic incumbent was Emmett Fitzpatrick, and one of his primary challengers was Ed Rendell. I liked what I heard Ed Rendell talking about on TV and the radio. I thought that if I could just get the chance to meet with him, even for a few minutes, I might be able to convince him that I would be a good addition to the office if he won the election. So I went to Rendell's campaign headquarters in Center City, Philadelphia, with my résumé and a hope that I could figure out a way to meet with the candidate himself.

When I got there I explained to Mr. Rendell's secretary that I wanted to talk with him for just five minutes if I could. She asked me what I wanted and I explained my mission to her. Her first reaction was somewhat curt: "Everyone wants to talk with Mr. Rendell. Have a seat. He'll be back sometime today but I have no idea when." So I waited. But I didn't just sit there. I asked her about her involvement with the campaign and what she thought of Mr. Rendell and how things were going. We talked about the photograph on her desk, which, as I recall, was a picture of her family. After a while I offered to put stamps on the envelopes she was mailing out. In short, we hit it off.

Four hours later, Mr. Rendell came in surrounded by his entourage. His secretary called over to him, "Hey, Ed, I've been talking with this young lady this afternoon and I like her. She wants to talk with you about a job." She had become a trusted contact in the four hours we had spent together. Rendell waved me into his office. I knew that I only had about five minutes to advocate for myself, so I launched into it. "Mr. Rendell, I have just finished law school and my dream is to be a prosecutor. I was a social worker before I went to law school, but I hope you won't hold that against me. I have been told that without a personal connection to someone in the district attorney's office I will never get in."

Rendell asked for my résumé, which he reviewed, and then said, "I can tell you will make a good prosecutor, and I don't intend to run the office hiring based on favoritism, but I have no idea whether I will win this election. So, tell you what, you leave your résumé with me, and if I do happen to win, send me a letter reminding me about this conversation, and you will have the chance to interview for a job if I am the next district attorney." I was delighted to hear this news. I am certain that if I had simply sent Mr. Rendell my résumé without a personal visit, I would not have had the same result.

Ed Rendell won the primary and then the general election, becoming district attorney. I sent him a letter reminding him of our conversation. I had an interview and landed my first job as a lawyer, becoming an assistant district attorney despite the odds.

One of the important lessons I learned about networking from this experience is that the trusted contact does not have to be a lifelong friend. I was open to talking with the seemingly ogre-like secretary, who proved to be a knight and a gatekeeper for the castle I sought to join. I also inadvertently adopted the six attitudes I have come to recognize as those that create greater luck for job seekers:

First, I thought outside the box by deciding to show up at campaign headquarters with my resume (Optimism/Opportunism). I was hoping to meet in person with Mr. Rendell (Interaction). I knew that the States Attorney's Office routinely hired from a pool of new graduates including graduates of my law school, so I should be part of a group of potential applicants the office would vet (Pragmatism). When I arrived at campaign headquarters, I found Mr. Rendell's secretary and even though she was not initially very friendly, I had a hunch that we might hit it off (Intuition). I stayed for hour hours waiting to meet for just a few minutes with Mr. Rendell (Tenacity). When we met I advocated for myself and it worked out well (Opportunism).

Looking at the elements of the formula for who gets a job, it is clear that these requirements were also satisfied:

1. The skill set that the prosecutor's office looked for was new graduates.
2. The trusted contact was Mr. Rendell's secretary.
3. The work was there.
4. The music was good.

A Creative Way to Meet Up with a Gatekeeper

Later in my career, when I wanted to be hired by the United States attorney's office in Chicago, I relied on creative networking again. By this time

I had been an assistant state's attorney for about three years in Philadelphia and then Chicago at the state's attorney's office in Cook County. I had gained experience doing hundreds of trials in state court and had developed investigations in the official misconduct unit, which is the state court skill set equivalent of the kinds of investigations and trials done by the U.S. attorney's office. I had applied to become a federal prosecutor, but my application seemed to be bogged down. I had not heard from the office to arrange an interview. After hearing that people with my experience in state court were hired by the office but that there were hundreds of applicants for a small number of positions, I decided to find a gatekeeper to support my efforts.

I learned that one of the gatekeepers was Senator Chuck Percy of Illinois. I had hoped to meet with Senator Percy by getting an introduction through a close friend's father. Unfortunately, my friend's father did not forward my résumé to Senator Percy even though he assured me he would do so. Months went by, and I decided that I needed to be more creative about meeting the senator.

I learned that Senator Percy was a tennis player, and that he played at the same courts where I played. I made it a point to find out when he would be there and showed up to play on the same court after he finished. As he left the court I went up to the senator, shook his hand and said, "Senator Percy, it's a pleasure to finally meet you. I've almost met you for the past four months." I explained that I had met his friend, that I had been hoping to get an introduction to talk about why I would make a terrific assistant U.S. attorney, and that I had the right background for the job. After talking with me briefly, the senator agreed to meet with me for an informal interview and asked me to bring my résumé. We talked for about twenty minutes, and I left my résumé with him. After that I received a letter inviting me to call to arrange an interview at the U.S. attorney's office. The interview went well, and I was hired for that job.

The reason this approach worked well had to do with the same key factors enumerated before.

1. My skill set was a match for the job.
2. I came to the attention of the senator and the U.S. attorney's office through a trusted contact.
3. There was work there.
4. The music was good in the interview.

When you try for a creative meet-up with a key person, you may be thrust immediately into an informal interview. Much will depend on the advocacy that you do in that meeting. Preparation for the interview is well worth the time you spend on it.

Showing Up in Person Without a Knight or Wizard to Introduce You

When I work with clients, I do not routinely encourage them to just show up on the doorstep of the workplace where they want to be hired. Despite that general advice, I have had a number of clients who are naturally comfortable with people and who have successfully used this tactic to eventually work in smaller workplaces that turned out to be open to such an approach.

One woman I worked with was trying to move from the practice of law to a related but nonlegal field involving work-life balance issues. She had gotten involved in activities supporting work-life balance in the law and saw an advertisement for a position that was the job of her dreams with a workplace she had heard good things about. She had actually kept clippings of articles about this workplace and their activities for many years. Armed with her convincingly yellowed newspaper articles in her file folder and her résumé, which she revised to highlight the background that fit with the position she sought, she showed up at the doorstep of that company and asked if she could speak to the person in charge of hiring.

In the informal interview that followed, she expressed her longstanding interest in the employer's mission and showed that person the file of articles she had kept. Even though other applicants had more appropriate skill sets, she landed that job. The reason her approach was effective was particularly because of the small size of the workplace (approximately 15 employees), her positive and assertive but not aggressive approach, and her evidence of prior longstanding interest in, engagement in, and knowledge of the field and their specific company.

Many gifted networkers land jobs by employing creative networking approaches such as engineered meetings that bring them to the attention of key people in situations that advance their quests. However, creative networking requires good judgment, planning, sensitivity, people skills, and some courage to think and act outside the box while exercising caution about conforming to workplace expectations and norms.

12 The Tipping Point and the Campaign Phase

There comes a time when you have enough information to know that there are a number of workplaces that might be job prospects for you.

This is the tipping point.

How Do You Know When You Have Reached the Tipping Point?

The tipping point occurs when you are ready to target particular workplaces you have vetted as prospects. It is important to identify this shift in your thinking, because if you are not certain about the way you view the workplace, you might end up inadvertently giving a key contact person the impression that you are not interested in that contact person's workplace. This is a little bit like the difference in the way you would talk to someone about dating as opposed to talking to someone about marriage. If you are still in a dating mode, you will be more likely to want to find out about other people to meet. If you want to get married, you do not talk about additional significant others because that would give the wrong message to your one and only.

You may have identified only one castle or you may know of a number of castles where you are ready to meet the keeper of the keys. The tipping point occurs somewhat unpredictably as you conduct your quest. You might discover early that a particular place would work well for you, but there may be a dozen more castles that will emerge as you keep networking. What that means is that you still need to keep up the quest. When you do find a castle you like, start your campaign for that workplace and continue your quest with others that you are still unsure about. Use your Essential Elements template to be sure the workplace matches your needs.

Can You Start at the Tipping Point Without Conducting a Quest?

If you are working with recruiters who find opportunities for you, you will jump over the quest phase and go immediately into the campaign phase. If you have sent a résumé in response to an ad and the dragon passes it along to the key keeper, you will go right into the campaign phase. Some people even begin their quests with enough knowledge to jump to the tipping point. They can bypass much of the quest. They might know this information because they have already been living in the neighborhood or they once were or are now part of the village surrounding the castle. It can also happen through the assistance of a powerful and friendly wizard who is willing to share her network with you.

Another way to jump to the campaign part of the quest is via a website posting. If you believe that your skill set matches or surpasses that of comparable candidates or people already working at targeted castles, you can try accessing the websites of firms and companies that your preliminary research indicates would be good matches for you to see if they are posting new jobs that require your skill set or skills that are reasonably close to yours. Some workplaces will vet you strictly on the strength of a website submission.

Although it might seem logical that overqualification—having more experience than requested or more variety of experience than requested in the ad—ought to be favorable for your candidacy, in fact the opposite may be true. When assessing your match for the workplace needs based on the website posting, be aware that more may not be better when it comes to years worked or experience gained. Nonetheless, if your background is close, you should apply and make your case in the interview.

What Do You Miss Out on If You Skip the Job Quest?

Developing Relationships with Knights and Wizards. When you jump immediately to the campaign phase, you miss out on all the knights and wizards you could have met on the road, with whom you would have created trust relationships and friendships that could lead to a stronger network for your future and marketing potential for a long lasting career in the law. These days, if you are in private practice and do not develop business, you will have to rely on those partners who can bring in business. You risk becoming a service partner, the handmaiden of the partner with portable practice. This is not a secure role. If that partner leaves the firm or retires, you may lose your source of work and become vulnerable for job loss. It is important to learn to be a rainmaker if you are planning to stay in private practice, and the networking you do in a job search can create that interpersonal foundation and help you to hone the marketing skills you will need in the future.

Learning Inside Information about the Market and Workplaces. If you go directly to the keeper of the keys, you will have an interview, and in that interview the key keeper and others, such as recruiters, will portray the workplace in a positive light. "Everyone is happy here. We all love it here." That information might not be accurate.

By conducting a quest, you will learn more inside information. The keeper of the keys might, for example, be a micromanager or a screamer, but he or she will not warn you about that. For example, the firm may be seeking a new lawyer because the partner overseeing the practice group has rage attacks and regularly demolishes associates' self-esteem. You would want to know that. The secretaries, paralegals and lawyers who used to work at this firm know how difficult this partner is to work for. Family members of current and past associates could tell you stories about this partner. People who are likely to spill the beans about the workplace are the ones who are not in the inner circle. They are loosely affiliated with the workplace. They are the spouses of the lawyers who work for the difficult partner. They are the lawyers who have left the firm and no longer have allegiance there. They are the secretaries, paralegals, and others who worked for that castle. When you tell people in the village that you are looking for places that are busy, active, growing, and *have a good reputation,* meaning where people like to work, you are checking out the workplace culture. People with loose or weak affiliations are more likely to be frank about what they have heard about the workplace culture and about individuals at a particular workplace.

Why You Can and Should Use the "J" Word Once You Reach the Campaign Phase

When you reach the tipping point you can use the "J" word. You can talk about your interest in a job at a particular castle and be direct about it with the knights and wizards, villagers and gatekeepers you encounter on your quest because you know where you want to land, you know you fit the profile of the kind of person the workplace likes to hire, there is work-flow, and now you want to come to the attention of the castle staff through a trusted contact if you can find a way to do it.

What Is an Endorsement and Why Is It Important?

The campaign phase of your job quest is your concerted effort to find the gatekeepers and the keeper of the keys to try to meet with them. You try to come to the attention of the workplace through trusted contacts, people who have credibility with the workplace you are vetting. You also want to make a concerted effort to elicit *endorsements* from your supporters.

An *endorser* has three qualities:

1. This person knows you, likes you, and knows your work.
2. This person knows someone in the castle or a gatekeeper for that castle.
3. This person is willing to vouch for you to someone in the hierarchy of the castle.

Sometimes people who could really assist your campaign to be hired do not realize how important they are to your success. These people might not think to ask you whether you would like them to vouch for you to the castle staff or the key keeper. If that is the case, do not be shy about asking for their help and explaining what you hope they will do to assist you. Ask for an endorsement.

Choose the right people to endorse you. There may be people who will agree to help you, but you might not benefit very much from their assistance. Choose people to do this important job for you based on their relationship to the workplace you are trying to connect with but also based on how positive and articulate they will be about you to the castle staff. Try to land endorsements from people who have good relationships with the key keeper and gatekeeper. Remember the three qualities of an endorser. A person who does not know you very well will not be able to give the most accurate picture of you to the key keeper or gatekeeper. Be careful not to ask a person who does not know your work for a recommendation that would include material knowledge about your work ethic or work product. Choose your endorsers carefully.

For example, if you ask a friend of a friend to say something good about you but that person has never worked with you or never met you in person, you cannot expect to receive a credible endorsement. The cure for this attenuated relationship might be to meet in person over lunch and give the individual a chance to vet you. That informal interview might convince him or her to introduce you to the key keeper.

The level of trust you enjoy from an endorsement can be an extension of positive feeling from the endorsing person to members of his close group on your behalf. For example, if you are a Notre Dame graduate and you find a supportive partner at your law firm who is also a Notre Dame graduate, who likes you and is willing to vouch for you and help you to meet some of his classmates, many who have become partners too, good will from your contact can transfer to you if you make a good impression. The same is true for other people with connectors into the workplace, such as professors who liked the research work you did for them, the judge you clerked for, the lawyer who ran the legal clinic at your school, or the head of the community service fundraiser you worked on.

If you have done good work in your student and professional lives, there are people who have been impressed. Now is the time to ask them to rally to your support. It is as if you are running for office and you ask your supporters to give you a hand if they are comfortable doing that. You are asking your supporters to vouch for you to their extended groups of friends and colleagues.

Social networks such as LinkedIn may also be helpful. You cannot, however, rely solely on an Internet friendship to elicit endorsements, because the level of trust is too attenuated and impersonal. Remember that the most effective endorsements come from people who know you, like you, and also know your work. People who can endorse you have interacted with you in person, seen your demeanor, observed you under pressure, watched you solve problems and make judgment calls, and they have liked what they have seen.

Ideally, when endorsers talk about you they speak from their "real time" experience with you. If you do not have that level of relationship, you might still create trust if you meet in person for breakfast, lunch, dinner, coffee, or in someone's office, and create a good impression. That connection is the equivalent of a strong informal interview, which can create support for your bid in your job campaign. That good impression includes giving back to your knight or wizard by giving the kinds of gifts described in Chapter 8: information, promotion, connection, attention, or an appropriate small tangible gift like a book.

How to Move from Quest to Campaign in an Informal Interview

There is another way to shift gears from the quest to the campaign phase. The shift occurs in the informal or informational interview.

Perhaps you have talked with a close friend and discussed your prototype workplaces and the neighborhoods you are looking for, and that friend has suggested that you meet with a contact of his who is in one of the right neighborhoods and is a nice person. You e-mail the contact, introduce yourself, and briefly describe the information you are looking for. You ask if he would be willing to talk with you. He says yes. You then briefly talk over the phone, and you can tell by the voice that you have a knight. You confirm a lunch.

You are now in the role of investigative reporter and new friend. You learn about his career and why he did what he did. In the process, you also ask questions and learn about where he works. You have been doing your research about places of interest and have learned about the various castles with potential in the neighborhood you seek to join. This contact is working at a firm you have already thought might have the potential to be a good fit for you. He describes what he does and says positive things about his firm. At that point a little voice in your head is saying, "I wish I could work there. I wish I could work there."

If you are thinking that, then use certain words to change the focus of the conversation from quest to campaign. What are those words?

"I have no idea if your workplace has a need for someone with my background, but I wonder if it makes sense to find out by starting a dialogue with whoever is in charge of hiring. Do you know who that is?"

With those simple but powerful words you have shifted the conversation's focus, and learned about the secret key keeper as well. You have opened up the possibility that you would be interested in a job at this workplace.

In the informational interview, the scent of "job" is in the air whether you intend it to be there or not. You do not have to say the word *job*, because the contact is aware of your ultimate agenda. The person you are talking with knows that your goal is to land a job at the right workplace and that you are on the hunt. Avoid insincerity. If you say you have one agenda (information) and you clearly have an ulterior motive (job), you may lose your connection's interest. Therefore, I recommend the following approaches for most people.

First, if you have set up an informational meeting, go into that meeting expecting only to learn more about the workplace, the neighborhood, the contact person, and the market in general. Rely on your contact as a career counselor and market advisor.

Then, if you have done your homework, you think that the workplace might be a good castle, you have become more excited about the workplace during the informational meeting, and you have learned that your background fits well, go ahead and speak up about your interest. Do not be afraid to move the discussion into the campaign phase. Hesitation on your part may be perceived as a lack of interest.

Finally, if you already know that the workplace where this contact is employed is one that is on your list of castles, reveal your interest in landing a job there earlier in the meeting. Move into the campaign phase when you learn that the workplace is busy, active, and growing. Use the magic words that shift the conversation from quest to campaign.

When Can You Move Immediately into the Campaign?

If you already know the type of workplace that matches your skill set and you have a neighborhood you are a part of or can tap into, you may be able to find out where the work is flowing within this circumscribed neighborhood by utilizing a rapid telephone or e-mail campaign for a relatively quick search.

You Know the Neighborhood Already

A young lawyer had been working for a boutique litigation firm for about three years, the last two working almost exclusively for a very difficult partner. This partner had a reputation for being extremely critical of his associates, many of whom left the firm vowing to leave the practice of law altogether because they were so demoralized. After a pretty good beginning with this partner, the associate ran afoul of him and was sentenced to outplacement. It was a blessing in disguise, since she had been hoping to find a way out of this difficult situation and wanted a different practice area niche as well. As is true with many associates, she did not have the time to search while she worked at the firm as the right-hand for this demanding partner.

The associate liked litigation. She wanted to move to a different litigation firm where she could get a fresh start in a different practice area with a more compatible partner. She had a pretty good idea of the comparable firms in town and had friends who were associates at many of these firms. She also had a wizard relative who was happy to help her out and a group of supportive partners at her old firm who liked her and were ready to say good things about her.

This associate was able to conduct a very quick search in the neighborhood she was qualified for in which she already had some contacts.

She conducted her job quest in textbook fashion by taking the following steps:

1. She met with the wizards including her relative and the supportive partners.
2. She described what she was looking for in very clear terms and told people her goal and problem.
3. She engaged in a telephone and e-mail campaign with her friends at comparable boutiques and asked for information about whether their firms were busy, growing, and good places to work.
4. She met in person with many of her knights and wizards, reinforcing their trust and friendship. Her contacts gave her new contacts at firms beyond her knowledge base. She met with them as well.

   During her search for a new job she worked full time and even left town for a brief trial, but by the second month of her search, she knew where she was likely to be hired and engaged

in a campaign to have her supporters endorse her to other key people at the firms where she was hoping to work.
5. She worked on her interview by doing a mock interview and thinking through strong answers and the anecdotal evidence to support her statements about herself.

She was hired at a litigation boutique in the practice area she had hoped to move into just two months and twenty days after she began her search.

You Tap into the Network of a Supportive Wizard

When I first came to Chicago after practicing as an assistant district attorney in Philadelphia for two years, I needed a part-time job to support myself while I studied for the Illinois bar exam. I tried to figure out where my skills would be useful in the Chicago market. At that point I had a masters degree in social work, a JD from Temple University, and two years of litigation practice as a prosecutor. I thought that maybe I would be especially helpful to a lawyer doing matrimonial law because of my counseling and litigation background.

I knew no matrimonial lawyers in Chicago, though I had been interested in the practice area and enjoyed my matrimonial law class in law school. I had recently read a book written by a divorce lawyer who practiced in Chicago, so I called his office. I got past the secretary by telling her that I enjoyed reading Mr. X's book and that I was a Philadelphia lawyer who had recently moved to Chicago. Perhaps the times were different then, but that was all I needed to say to be able to talk directly to this lawyer.

I began by telling Mr. X how much I enjoyed his book and quickly articulated my situation, namely that I hoped to find a part-time job in matrimonial law while studying for the bar exam. I gave him a thumbnail sketch of my skills, said good things about myself, and explained why I wanted to find a part-time job doing matrimonial law. I said I didn't know if he had a need for someone with my background, but if he didn't, could he think of anyone else practicing matrimonial law who might need some extra help?

He told me he didn't need any help, but there were a few guys in town he could name who might like to have some assistance on a part-time basis. He began to list them and gave me some inside information about a number of them: this one was a barracuda and that one was expanding his firm and that other one was really a great guy but had gotten too busy and he could really use a hand whether he thought so or not.

What was surprising to me was his willingness to reveal so much about people and firms without knowing me. As he spoke, I simply encouraged him to say more by expressing my interest and joining with him around his remarks. When he said, "I have no idea why this guy is so disorganized, but I think it's only going to get worse," I asked, "Really? Why is that?" And he replied, "Because next year he's supposed to be the head of the matrimonial law committee for the bar association, and I have no idea how he's going to get everything done!"

Some people call this schmoozing, or small talk. But it's also something like the tactic you would employ in a good direct exam. You draw people out and encourage them to say more. The more they say, the more you learn. The more you join with them, the more they develop a comfort level with you. An ability to create a comfort level with new people you encounter is the essence of effective networking.

After I was done talking with this gregarious and helpful lawyer, I had the names of about five other matrimonial lawyers who were friends of his that he insisted I call, and I had learned useful gossip about each one of them. "Call them up and tell them I sent you. Now don't say I vouch for your work, of course, but tell them we talked over the phone and tell them what you are looking for. I'm sure you'll find a part-time job for the summer if you do this."

So, with his blessing, I began calling his friends in this neighborhood of matrimonial lawyers, and I was amazed that I was able to talk with most of them by using the first lawyer's name, as he had instructed me to do. I was very clear about the fact that he did not vouch for my work, but I had various judges and supervisors in Philadelphia who would be happy to recommend me. I called about twenty lawyers in two days and got to talk with about a dozen of them. In each case they were friendly and helpful and educated me about this village of matrimonial lawyers, giving me more names of lawyers who might need help along with a brief description of each person. In each case they were willing to gossip with me once they knew who had advised me to call.

By the second day, I had learned from more than one source about a lawyer who was generally described as a great guy who was overworked and in need of help because his practice was so successful. When I called him up on the second day of my quest, I mentioned that I had heard about him from other lawyers, who I named, and that all of them said I should call because he was so busy and maybe he could use some extra help for the summer. He laughed and said, "Why don't you come down to my office tomorrow? Maybe with your counseling background you can tell me why so many of my clients act as crazy as they do."

I met with him the next day, and we put together a part-time job to meet his needs and my needs. He was a truly wonderful guy, just as the other lawyers described.

Why did this search take only three days? Because I was invited to piggyback on the network of a wizard who was well connected in the neighborhood and willing to allow me to use those connections. He was not only nice enough to share his network with me, he taught me a lot about how good networking is accomplished. Later, when I called him back to thank him, he told me that helping me to network was also a favor he did for his friends in the field. "And when you do a good job," he said, "that guy's going to thank me for helping him out." What goes around comes around.

Today this search might have to be a combined telephone and e-mail search. I would have tried to connect by phone, but if that did not work I would have used e-mail, always mentioning the trusted contact in the subject line and the first line of the body of the letter. I would have asked this helpful wizard if he would be willing to send a brief e-mail to the people he recommended to me indicating that I would be contacting them, so that my e-mail would not get blocked by the spam filter. I would have tried to move from e-mail to phone to in-person meeting.

How to Campaign for a Job You Create

There are times when it is possible to actually create a position for yourself where there was no job previously. The job is created because the work is there and your skill set matches the needs of the workplace. It also helps if one or two of the people who would endorse you already work there. You may need to produce a proposal to help key keepers and others to feel comfortable with the decision to create a new position and then to hire you to do it.

A client I worked with a few years ago was a partner at a midsized firm and did work for a growing not-for-profit. As the not-for-profit grew, so did the complexity of its legal issues. This partner continued to handle most of the work, relying on others in the firm to address areas of law that were not his practice area. As time went on, this partner came to me for advice about how to wind down his career. He was ready to move out of the firm and did not need to make the same amount of money anymore, but he did not want to leave the practice of law altogether. He wanted to find work that was more meaningful to him, where, he said, "I can really feel good about the mission."

After some discussion we agreed that he should try to convince the not-for-profit that trusted him already to consider bringing him in-house. He could save them money, and he already had a strong relationship with the keeper of the keys and other insiders. He put together a proposal to show the board how he could help them trim their budget by bringing him in-house. He understood the company's history, their problems, and their legal needs. He also understood how law firms work and could oversee pricing and litigation done by outside counsel. He was the ideal candidate for this yet-to-be-created position.

The not-for-profit considered his request for a "to-be-created" job. The request was championed by the head of the not-for-profit, which made it more likely to be successful. Before hiring him, they advertised the position on their website, but this job listing was not really a viable position. The ad was a necessary step to satisfy protocol, but the job was already essentially taken by an insider—my client, who had created the position and led a successful campaign to land it.

There may also be an opportunity to create a job for yourself by approaching a workplace with a creative proposal or ideas that will help the company to be more successful. This usually works better in a business context and is less effective for lawyers seeking traditional jobs as lawyers. However, the creative proposal might work well if a job-seeking lawyer is approaching a consulting firm or trade association or some other less traditional job where background as a lawyer is an asset. If you take the time to study the company and approach the entity with a business idea, be sure you take steps to protect your creative effort, with a copyright, for example, before sharing it with the potential employer.

13 Common Pitfalls and How to Avoid Them

When I present this quest-to-campaign networking approach to clients and send them out to conduct their searches, I set up another session after a few weeks to see how they are doing. Some of my clients come to the session beaming. They have uncovered a number of good opportunities or are hearing about some places with potential. Some of them are into the interview phase or are deciding between a number of job options. But not everyone has an easy time of it. Here are some of the common pitfalls that job seekers may encounter.

Failing to Direct and Guide Your Knights and Wizards

The single biggest problem I hear about when clients return to describe their quest status is a failure to work closely with the knights and wizards to guide them to provide the needed search information. Many of the well-meaning people you meet with as you conduct your quest have been asked to give other people help in their job quests. And those other people have asked for advice and information about where the jobs are. You can't blame your contacts for thinking that that is the information you want also.

Unless you guide your knights and wizards clearly, you run the risk that these people will fall back into job-finder mode and try to provide you with overly brief information about jobs they have heard about, not where the work is flowing, not descriptions of workplaces that fit your needs or other on-the-ground information you are looking for. It is up to you to patiently go back and describe again the information you seek.

Another potential hazard in the quest process is failing to walk the contact person through descriptions of the workplaces you seek. You might have identified three different types of workplaces that would be good matches for you. One might be a midsize firm doing litigation, another could be in-house overseeing litigation, and another might be a government job doing investigations and litigation. Guiding your advisors works best if you clearly identify each option, label each one (option 1, 2, and 3), and then clearly address each one with your contact separately, going through key aspects of each before moving on to the next.

The reason you have to do this is because of the *treasure chest concept*—you do not know who your contact knows, even if you think that you do. You have to check each time and get each box open one at a time with each knight or wizard you talk with.

Failing to Provide Clear Prototypes

All too often the job seeker is either not clear enough or too detailed about the opportunity sought. Lack of clarity can be confusing to a contact person who is trying to help out by suggesting places that fit the description the job seeker is giving. Be clear enough to prompt an idea of workplaces that match the descriptions in the minds of your contacts without ruling out too many potentially good workplaces.

An example of how this relates to job search comes from a client of mine who wanted to do criminal defense work at a law firm. He had been at a large firm, so as he conducted his networking he described only large workplaces to his contact people. He failed to include boutiques in his descriptions, so his contacts did not recommend any smaller firms, even though some boutiques might have been a very good match for his needs. By being too narrow about the size of the workplace, he may have lost out on opportunities that might have been right for him.

Another client was overly narrow in his description of what he wanted to find. He said he would like a job in a corporation overseeing product liability litigation. But his background in litigation made him a good candidate for many other opportunities. He ended up in a government job with the postal service, but his search took longer than he had hoped, perhaps because he started out with a more narrow focus.

Failing to Move Beyond Biography

Another common mistake job seekers can make is to be stuck in the role of biographer when talking with their knights and wizards. Often these networkers understand that networking is about friendship and they take that to heart, but they sometimes engage the contact person in a long conversation that does not advance beyond the contact person's biography.

This is appropriate when the networking is purely informational and the goal is to find a better fitting career direction. But for a job quest, the information you need goes beyond biography. It is very important to obtain market knowledge as well as convey clear information about the kind of workplace you are trying to learn about. You need to guide your contact to the topics you want to learn about and ask for advice, information, market knowledge, the names of more knights and wizards, and whether you can name your contact to open the door with these additional contact people. You also want to ask whether this contact person would be willing to send an e-mail explaining why you are going to be following up with a phone call to those additional people.

Using the "J" Word Too Soon

We have seen that the mention of the word *job* early in your networking can have a chilling effect and might limit the effectiveness of your search. Although it is true that you are looking for a job, attempts to talk about jobs and where they are will often stunt the conversation and limit the knowledge you obtain. Instead of using the "J" word early in your networking efforts, focus instead on creating a viable trust relationship in which there is give and take. Ask for advice, information, and market knowledge. Engage your natural counselor-contact person in a topic that requires advice. Do not let others take the role of being your recruiter unless you have great faith that they will not drop the ball. Make the focus of your discussion the master list of people and places you have developed, and ask for ideas about more people and places to add to your list.

Allowing an Ogre to Defeat You

Although most people are well meaning and helpful, there are a handful of people you will encounter in your quest who will not be so. They may even start out seeming to be helpful knights or wizards, but at some time they change into ogres. They might tell you that your search is not going to be productive; they might give you bad advice; they might put you down in some way. If you encounter someone who puts a damper on your enthusiasm or who tells you that you have no chance to get a certain kind of job, take that opinion under advisement. Do your homework. Be sure that your credentials are close enough to the workplace need, for example. Understand the odds you face. But do not let an ogre defeat you.

Running Back to the Cottage to Send Résumés to Dragons

Quests are not easy; that's why they are heroic. They are time consuming and require courage and energy, but the payoff is great. Not only do you land the job you know you want because you have defined what you are searching for, but you develop wonderful friends during your journey. Some of them will join your round table, and many will become your sources of business as your career moves forward. There are, however, some job seekers who venture into the forest briefly, only to run back to the safety of their cottages, sending résumés to castles as their primary method of job search. There is nothing wrong with continuing to watch for jobs on the Internet that appear to be great matches for you, unless it becomes an overly time-consuming activity. There is nothing wrong with checking websites of the firms and companies that your research tells you would be great matches for you. There is nothing wrong with checking in from time to time with recruiters to see whether they will work with you based on any recent orders they have to fill. But if you do not conduct a networking job quest at all, you miss too much of the hidden job market, limit your effectiveness, and miss out on the long-term career benefits of meeting people in your legal neighborhood.

Failing to Explore Alternative Arrangements

There can be many reasons for a slow search. A poor economy will yield fewer jobs simply because the work is not flowing well. Searches can take longer because employers are nervous about hiring anyone until they trust the sustainability of the work-flow. In that case, the employer may hope to increase the productivity of the current staff and avoid new hiring as long as possible. In such instances, the potential employer may be more open to the idea of temporary assistance, independent contracting, or part-time help. These arrangements can be suggested by the job seeker and explored with the employer, because it is a way to get a foot in the door. And that can lead to a job.

To that end, failing to explore possible alternative arrangements with the potential employer is a common job search mistake. The job seeker thinks, "If I do not get the opportunity for a full-time job right away, I need to move along in my search." Very often, however, a lawyer who creates a relationship with a workplace by starting out in a nontraditional role may be able to add value to the workplace and parlay the alternative arrangement into a full-time job. The lawyers who are most successful at making this shift to full time generally try to create relationships with other key lawyers at the workplace while doing outstanding work. Not all workplaces will be open to this shift from alternative track to full-time job, but even if that is not going to happen, the job seeker is getting experience and additional skills, not to mention making some money.

Contract Work

If the market is particularly difficult, you may need to start out by suggesting that you are willing to do contract work or temporary work. Asking for a nontraditional arrangement that might turn into a traditional job if you do well typically works best with smaller to midsize firms that do not have as much structure in place. If you are a new graduate, consider trying to do an internship to get in the door and start building the skill set you need, with an expectation that you will be considered for a more traditional position after a specified period of time. The small to midsize firms might be interested in that arrangement.

Some larger workplaces are using contract lawyers to do document review in larger numbers than ever before. Often they find these contract lawyers through an agency that places temporary workers. There are lawyers who like the freedom of contract or temporary work. The workload is usually fairly predictable, if rote, and there is little stress. Lawyers who like this kind of position often highly value lifestyle and work/life balance. Other lawyers are not satisfied with the limited nature of contract or temporary work and are disappointed with the limited skill set they can develop at these jobs on a long-term basis.

14 A Model Quest

The secret of how luck works is important to demystify so that every-one trying to find jobs can benefit from the natural networkers. To that end, it is useful to deconstruct a model search in order to study the components of luck and chance and see how they combined with motivation and clear-eyed assessment to generate options for one job seeker.

*A*t the beginning of the recent recession, I received a call from a law firm asking if I could take a referral for outplacement of a fourth-year associate in the estate planning group. I met with this law-yer a few days later and learned about her background.

Agnes (not her real name) was the first-born child of hard-working Russian immigrants who had come to the United States while she was in junior high school. She worked hard in high school and attended a good state university where she majored in economics and gradu-ated with honors. After graduation she became a financial advisor at an investment firm. At this firm she handled internal legal issues and compliance issues, counseling clients and working with in-house legal counsel. She thoroughly enjoyed accommodating clients' needs and fielding financial questions. She felt most engaged when she helped cli-ents one-on-one.

She kept that job for three years and then attended a second-tier law school, where she graduated with honors and a 3.5/4.0 GPA. While in law school, she found her tax courses particularly interesting and went on to get an LL.M. in tax. She graduated with highest honors.

After graduation, she took a position with a well-respected, relatively large firm. She stayed there for two years. However, the firm lost a key rainmaker when he moved to a different firm and took his clients with him. Since Agnes's work as an associate depended on business from this partner, she was affected by the consequent loss of the business he brought in. The firm referred her to me for outplacement.

When I first met with Agnes, she told me that she had already been actively trying to find a job for a few weeks. She was doing a combination of searching on the Internet and interacting with people in the neighborhoods she thought might turn out to be fruitful.

Agnes had already figured out the key legal neighborhoods that might yield good results for her, given her skills and background, where the work-flow would be likely, and where she could engage in client counseling, which was her strength. She correctly figured out that, with the stock market falling drastically, many people would be concerned about wealth management and would want to be certain about how to protect whatever assets they had as well as protect their wealth for the next generation. She talked with people in that neighborhood to check her instincts. Many agreed with her assessment and verified that wealth management was a hot area, becoming hotter as a result of the collapse of the up side of the market.

Knowing this, she then looked at the villages that made the most sense for her and were likely to need help. She came up with three: 1) banks, 2) accounting firms, and 3) boutique law firms with corporate and estate planning practices. Then she launched her job quest.

Agnes had been an outstanding associate at her firm, and many of the partners there were happy to assist her. She met with them and worked with them to identify people and places that fit the villages she thought would be good bets. These partners turned out to be very helpful and provided her with names of people for networking purposes as well as law firms that fit the description she gave them.

She also tried to work with recruiters, but few recruiters were being asked to do associate searches because of the recession. She realized that she was on her own, but instead of getting depressed about that, she seemed to step up the pace of her networking interactions in an effort to learn more and work her search harder.

Agnes reworked her résumé and did a series of mock interviews to prepare for networking interviews. She learned how to conduct a productive networking search. She already seemed to understand most of the concepts, but she told me that it was helpful to verify that she was doing the right things in her search, because no one had ever taught her to do this and she wasn't sure she was doing her networking the right way. She also changed some of her networking activities, such as delaying the use of the "J" word until she had identified places she knew could be good prospects for her, engaging in longer in-person meetings with contact people, and using prototypes to help contacts identify good workplace prospects for her.

She was fearless about finding knights and wizards. She considered ogres to be calculated nuisances. She was undaunted about meeting with anybody and everybody. She instinctively knew when to ask for the endorsement from supportive partners. Her search efforts also stood out because of the energy and positive mindset she brought to her search, as well as her willingness to try out new ideas.

Agnes learned of a smaller firm with the wealth management practice area she had figured out was going to grow, driven by client need. She approached the firm by asking a supportive partner who knew good people at that firm to open the door for her, which he did. She was invited to meet with key partners for lunch, which turned out to be her informal interview. She continued her networking search and uncovered an interesting prospect at a bank. She kept the law firm informed about her other prospect, which probably made the firm nervous that they might lose her. They extended her an offer.

Almost exactly one month to the day after we met for the first session, Agnes landed the job she sought at the boutique law firm she had targeted. She also uncovered three other excellent prospects that either did or probably would have become job offers had she declined the offer from the law firm. No doubt part of her success was due to the fact that the failure of the economy on the up side of the market generated workflow on the down side of the market in the form of asset protection for future generations, and Agnes had the skill set to help clients with that problem. But she is also the kind of natural networker who lands on her feet.

I am certain that if she had been in a different practice area, she would have found her way to the work-flow, rewritten her résumé to reflect her skills in that practice area, and networked just as effectively to land a good job.

15 Concluding Remarks

We have come to the end of our journey together, and by now I hope you are more confident about what you need to do to have a productive job search. By now you think of your job search as a quest—a heroic journey. You are the hero, setting out into the forest to find your way to the castles that could be good for you, your search progressing from trusted contact to trusted contact.

You now have different attitudes about how to think about your job search, and a host of ideas about how to proceed and make this quest productive not only in helping you find a new job, but in helping you find your round table—a group of people who will support you for your entire career.

These alterations in thinking add to your luck. They can maximize good luck because you understand that what you might have thought of as a lucky or chance encounter has emanated from your efforts, your intuitive judgment, and your awareness of how the process of a job search works. As a result you can generate more lucky encounters.

One of my clients had an experience that underscores this point. He had reached the point in our work where he had the job quest session and had identified a number of firms that were good matches for his skill set and background and fit with his career goals. He brainstormed with me about how to connect with key people who could advance his quest. He mentioned that the local bar association was having a lunch meeting on a topic that was central to his practice area, but one that he already knew a lot about. I suggested that he go to this meeting, even if the information he would learn there might not be so important for him. He resisted at first, saying that he had a lot of work to do. But he did not rule it out.

When I met with him next he reported that he had gone to the meeting. "You will never guess who was sitting nearby !" he told me. "It was an old friend of mine. We got to talking and it turns out he is a good friend of one of the partners at one of the firms I told you about. He's going to help me out by introducing me to this partner. The three of us are going to lunch next week. I can't believe my luck!"

I agreed that this was a wonderful turn of events, but I didn't agree that it was just luck. He had set the stage for luck to happen for him. He had already identified the firms and people he wanted to connect with. He went to the meeting that he did not think would be helpful, but, since he took the approach that *you never know if there could be a treasure chest somewhere*, he went to the meeting in the spirit of trying to meet more knights and wizards. He talked with his friend in a way that elicited the information he needed. The fates did not conspire to cause this amazing result. He did. Why not take some credit?

If job seekers are motivated, know what to do and how to do it, and persevere with a sense of undaunted purpose, humor, curiosity, and concern for others, they make luck happen.

You can do this. You know what to do. You know how to prepare before you leave on your adventure: identify your career needs, find the work-flow, redo your résumé, and do research about the castles. You are armed with your computer, so you can continue to do research as you wend your way through the woods. You are ready to strike out on your journey, over the mountains and through the forest where you will meet many engaging and interesting characters, knights and wizards who will help you and become your friends and help you to find the gatekeepers and key keepers. You know how to help them in return. You know how to ask the right questions to find your way to the villages surrounding the castles and evade the dragon at the drawbridge by taking the path to the side door or the back door where you find villagers.

You know about ogres and how to keep them from stopping you. You know that you may have to fight the urge to retreat to the safety of your cottage.

When you have figured out the castles and know which ones may be able to use your help, you know you will need to launch your campaign to have your supportive friends speak up on your behalf and link you to the gatekeepers and key keepers in these castles. This is the time to use the word *job* and ask for endorsements. You will ace the interviews because you are prepared and you have recruited yourself to a workplace for which you are a good match.

This is your quest. You are in charge. Create your own *good luck!*

Appendix A — Find Your Career Sweet Spot

This appendix provides details on two important tools for finding your perfect job:

1. *AILS Assessment*
2. *Essential Elements Assessment*

AILS Assessment

Who should do the AILS assessment?

You should do an AILS assessment if one of these describes your situation:

1. You are not satisfied with your current career or job and you do not know why.
2. You are a new graduate and you are trying to figure out the best practice area to move into.
3. You have been let go because your practice area is overstocked with lawyers, and you want to find another direction for your career.

Who does not need to do the AILS assessment? If you already like your career/job/practice area and know you want to continue in this area, then you can skip to Essential Elements.

1. Aptitudes

What do you do well?

Most people excel when they are performing certain types of work and engaging in certain types of activities that play to their strengths. For example, some people are naturally good at math or science, while others are not as good at thinking that way. Some people are excellent logical, linear thinkers. Some people write well. Some people are good at understanding how other people think and are sensitive to nuances in human behavior. *Aptitudes* are our innate strengths and abilities.

For a job to be satisfying and a career path to be highly successful for you, it helps if your work can utilize your strong suits. If you are innately good at what you do, you will be more likely to be satisfied and successful at work.

Think back over your life to identify your aptitudes. Include those that your teachers, friends, and family have identified. Are you the person everyone talks to because you are easy to connect with? Are you the person in the center of a group and you enjoy the spotlight? Are you the person who wants to help others? Are you the person who everyone expects to get the right answer on the history exam? Sometimes other people can see our personal strengths more clearly than we can, so ask friends and family to add to this list if you need help.

APTITUDES

1. _____

2. _____

3. _____

4. _____

5. _____

6. _____

7. _____

8. _____

9. _____

10. _____

2. Interests

Interests are not necessarily the same as aptitudes.

What is an interest? It's the thing that gets you out of bed in the morning. You really look forward to doing this activity or thinking about this topic. For some people, it's a passionate excitement about something. For others, it is a strong interest in something. And for others it's a sense of fulfillment or engagement that does not rise to a level of passion or even strong interest, but when doing the activity the person enjoys life more.

To have a satisfying career we want to have an interest in what we are engaged in doing. It is not possible for a job to be totally interesting all of the time, however—that is why they call it *work* and pay people to do a *job*. But if there is a very low level of interest in any aspect of the work we do, and there is nothing else in the work setting that captures our interest, then the job will not be very gratifying. Interests can include such things as spending time with people we enjoy interacting with; the process of learning how to be a better courtroom lawyer; or learning how to put together a deal. Even if the work itself is not interesting to us (for example, document review), but we really enjoy the people we are working with and the fact that we can have a very full life outside of work, that counts.

In this exercise, try to list your strong interests. If you have an interest in having a life that includes many activities that you engage in outside of the workplace setting—training for a marathon, helping out at a shelter for battered women, learning karate, teaching Sunday school, traveling, writing fiction—list them as well. If you are strongly motivated to engage in activities outside of work, you might need to plan to have a job that allows you to have time for these activities.

Another way to figure out your interests is to imagine all of the magazines in the world are on a table in front of you. What would you pick to read about? Where do you spend your browsing time on the Internet? Do you read blogs? Which ones? What topics interest you? What do you gravitate to?

There are many people whose strongest interest is in having time with friends and family outside of work. For some people, that interest is a passion, especially if they are raising young children, for example. That passion might shift as the children get older, but it is an intense interest during the childrearing years. That interest should go on the list below.

It can trump everything else and is just as valid as any other passion or strong interest.

Finally, are you interested in the law? Do you like thinking legal thoughts? If not, that is important. Many people go into the field of law for other reasons. They are encouraged by friends and family. They want to make money. They do not know what else to do. But the practice of the law will require that you spend time understanding rules, regulations, precedents, cases, and statutes. You will read many legal documents and analyze them for content and compliance with the law. You will probably prepare many legal documents as well. To be a successful lawyer, you should like learning about the law and practicing law. That sounds simplistic, but it is remarkable to me as a career counselor how many lawyers I have worked with who really do not like thinking about the law. If you lack that basic interest, if you do not put "reading or thinking about the law" on your list of interests, that is a very important piece of information about yourself that may lead you to consider leaving the direct practice of law for a career that does engage your interests.

The transition to that new career might be made through a portal that is law-related, such as legal publishing, administrative work for a law school, marketing for a law firm, public relations for a legal entity, legal recruiting, development of a line of business apparel for women lawyers, or sales for a legal services provider like Westlaw, for example.

Always try to follow your interests when planning your career moves.

INTERESTS

List your interests and rate them on the scale by circling the number that reflects your level of interest (10 is the highest, and the same rating can be used for more than one interest).

1. _____   1_____5_____10

2. _____   1_____5_____10

3. _____   1_____5_____10

4. _____   1_____5_____10

5. _____   1_____5_____10

6. _____   1_____5_____10

7. _____   1_____5_____10

8. _____   1_____5_____10

9. _____   1_____5_____10

10. _____   1_____5_____10

(There is no magic number of interests to include on this list. Some people have only 2 or 3 and others have more than 10.)

3. Lifestyle

Our work needs to support the lifestyle we require to be happy. Lifestyle includes the amount of money we want to make and the work-life balance equation.

Some people are content to make $40,000, and others will not feel accomplished unless they make $600,000 or more. And there are plenty of people who envision a lifestyle that is sustainable on a compensation level that lies in between these extremes. In fact, the lower your salary expectation, the more your career options open up.

Lifestyle also includes the issue of balance between work and life outside of work. Many people need a work-life balance that is hard to find in a hard-charging environment such as a large law firm in a large city. There are many settings for the practice of law, however. Some of these settings are in small towns, others are in government, and others are in companies, trade associations, or not-for-profits. A better match of lifestyle needs to the workplace setting and compensation level can add to career satisfaction.

How do you envision the relationship between your ideal life and your work life? Even if you cannot achieve the best match right away, you can plan for a career that will help you to achieve a match in the future. You might need to pay off your student loans by going to a large firm and working extremely long hours for a period of time, but your long-term plan could include a move to a small town or a government job after a few years of practice; both of those tend to have somewhat more reasonable hours and often, but not always, less stressful settings.

If you have a long-range career goal of working something closer to a 40- to 50-hour week, you will want to enter a practice area at the large firm that will enhance that career transition in the future. Be careful to choose a firm that lets you have a say in the practice group you join, and try to pick a specialty that is valuable in government or in small firm practice. For example, you might choose estate planning because you can transition eventually to a small firm where that knowledge will enhance your value. You might try to work on government contracts at a large firm with an eye to gaining traction for an eventual move into government. These are just two ideas; there are countless others.

LIFESTYLE

Using the space below, write out a description of the life you want to have. Include the type of family you want, your home life, your outside activities, your interest in travel, as well as your aspirations in terms of your legal career.

4. Self-Actualization

Our workplaces shape us. The culture of the workplace, our colleagues, the activities we do to fulfill the requirements for our jobs, the people we interact with who are our clients and our bosses, the amount of time we spend alone or with others—these and many other elements in the work setting affect the person we are and are becoming.

There is a certain amount of plasticity in people in terms of how we grow as individuals. For example, if you need to pay attention to minute details for your job, you will probably get better at picking up small discrepancies not only at work but outside of work. If you need to be outspoken in a courtroom to be effective, you are likely to become more forceful in your dealings with people generally, even outside of the workplace. If you are a judge and you not only can but must interrupt people to move cases along, you are more likely to carry that behavior over into the world at large, even your social life. People learn behaviors that become part of their personalities for better or worse.

In addition, the experiences we have at work with co-workers and bosses, clients, opposing counsel, courtroom or other personnel, can and often will shape our behavior as well as our view of ourselves. For example, if you are a young lawyer doing the best you can to learn how to do your job, but you are consistently given negative feedback by your partners, that negative interaction can affect your sense of self-worth and self-esteem. Instead of becoming more competent over time, you might become more and more uncertain and even turn into a procrastinator, afraid to begin work on a project for fear it will not turn out well.

Think of every workplace as a unique mixture of people, workplace culture, and work that needs to be done. If you do this, you can imagine that the people who work in that particular setting will be affected by that particular environment. To make matters more complex, however, every person is also unique. Two people in the very same workplace might react very differently to events and situations. For example, a woman working in a small office with a number of men who tell dirty jokes and laugh about their sexual exploits might well experience that workplace as offensive and even intolerable. She might have actionable grounds for a harassment lawsuit. But if another man joining that same group feels comfortable talking about his own sexual exploits, he might find the workplace to be not only tolerable, but very collegial. People are unique and will react differently to a workplace.

What this means is that you have to figure out for yourself how your workplace is affecting you. It does not matter that you have certain sensitivities. That is just who you are. But given who you are, what is happening to you?

If you are someone who values honesty and prides yourself on being ethical, but your job calls for you to engage in devious tactics or hide the truth, that is probably affecting you in a negative way.

If you are a team-oriented person who loves interaction with others but your job requires that you spend 90% of your time alone in front of a computer doing research, and no one in the office says hello or smiles or talks with you, that is probably affecting you in a negative way.

If you are working in a place where you are valued and listened to, your opinion matters, and you have developed some expertise, you are probably becoming more confident not only as a lawyer, but as a person in general in the world outside of work.

How is your workplace shaping you? How are you responding to the people and the work you are doing? Do you like the person you are becoming? What is working for you? What is not working for you?

SELF-ACTUALIZATION

Use these pages to write down the ways the workplace is hurting you and/ or helping you to become the person you want to be.

For example: your goal is to become the best trial lawyer you can be. Is your workplace helping or hurting your ability to achieve this goal? If you never get into court, your workplace is currently hurting your achievement of that goal. But the workplace is helping you to obtain your goal if you have a lot of opportunities to try cases and get mentored.

Here is another illustration: you want to have a mission of helping other people in need, but the workplace is all about helping clients get more money. and that is not a mission that fires you up. The workplace is hurting your ability to achieve your goal.

Here is another illustration: you want to be a powerful person who gets things done. The workplace is giving you the opportunity for a lot of responsibility and you are getting more self-confident. Here the workplace is helping you to be all that you can and want to be.

Identify the important personal goals you have for yourself and write down whether your job is helping or hurting your ability to be the person you want to be.

Goal 1. _____

    Hurting?

    Helping?

Goal 2. _____

    Hurting?

    Helping?

Goal 3. _____

    Hurting?

    Helping?

Goal 4. _____

    Hurting?

    Helping?

Goal 5. _____

    Hurting?

    Helping?

Goal 6. _____

    Hurting?

    Helping?

Now that you have done these exercises, take a minute to review what you have learned. How closely matched are your aptitudes, interests, lifestyle needs, and personal goals with your current career/job? Overall, are you well matched for your current career/job?

If you have at least some satisfaction in all four categories—aptitude, interest, lifestyle, and self-actualization—you are doing okay. If one or more of these categories is missing the mark for you, you may need to work on changing your responsibilities somewhat, adding more of one kind of work and doing less of the sort of work you do not do as well or have less of an interest in doing. This exercise can help you figure out what you need to shift or tweak.

If, on the other hand, you are totally lacking one or more of these basic elements of career satisfaction, it is likely that you are dissatisfied with your career, and unless you change your practice area, your workplace, the type of job you do, or another key component of your work situation, you will be likely to continue to experience your work life in a negative way. Many people who are missing one or more of these four elements of career satisfaction are wearing out their loved ones by complaining about how unhappy they are. This exercise can help you at least start to identify where the dissatisfaction is coming from.

The next exercise, Essential Elements, will help you to more closely identify and hone a career direction that will be a better fit.

Essential Elements

You should do the Essential Elements exercise if one of the following decribes your situation:

1. You do not enjoy your current job/career and want to find a better fit.
2. You have more than one choice of job and you want to check to be sure you are choosing a job that matches your needs reasonably well.
3. You are starting a job search and you want to make sure you are looking for a job that suits your needs reasonably well.

Who does not need to do the Essential Elements exercise? Anyone who already knows that the current job/career is working well for him or her and is conducting a job search for the same kind of job that s/he had before.

What Is the Essential Elements Exercise?

Every person has a unique set of building blocks or elements that help him or her to have a satisfying career and enjoy their work-life. These building blocks are such things as a need for a mission that motivates you, control over your hours, a collegial group and a team approach to work, and many others. These elements will be different for each person. If you can identify what you need from your job, you will be in a better position to conduct a job search for a position that will meet your needs. This exercise helps you to identify the building blocks of a career that will be more sustaining for you by creating a template for a job that works well for you personally. Once you have this template, you can vet your potential job for your needs, and you will be more likely to find work that will satisfy you and in which you will excel.

The Essential Elements exercise helps you to design your search strategy and find the right job, but some people need to start with a work history to figure out what the elements are. Other people already have a good grasp of what those elements are.

If you need help to identify the elements you need in your work life to be happy, start with a Work History (see page 153).

If you already have a good idea of the elements you need to have to be satisfied with your job, start with Essential Elements (see page 156).

Work History

List work you have done, paid or unpaid, whether or not it was termed a "job." Include internships, work you did for fundraising events, and volunteer work of any kind, and include college and law school on the list of work you have done.

Under each work entry make a list of what you liked and did not like about the work. Include your reaction to the people, the hours, the type of work you did, and anything else about the job or work that stands out in your mind.

Use the following format to create your work history. It is good to cover every position you have ever had, but you can lump early jobs together. For example, if you had many waitressing jobs or camp counselor jobs and your experience in each instance were similar, you can group them under one heading.

Here is an example of a work history:

Job: Working at Joe's Fish Place as a server

+	−
Loved the people I worked with	The pay was awful
Great customers	I didn't like the fast pace
Hours were good	Stressful at times when too busy
When work was over I was done— I didn't take work home with me	

Job: Project Assistant for a small firm doing plaintiff's personal injury

+	−
Liked research and writing a lot	The work was sort of boring
Really respected the lawyers	I did not get to interact with clients and help them
Liked the lawyers I worked for	The mission didn't do much for me (personal injury)
I knew I what I was supposed to do	
I didn't bring work home at night	

Job: Undergrad Student

+	−
Loved college!	Studying for exams was awful too stressful!!
Independence	
Learning new things	
Great people	
Some terrific professors	
Great parties	
Relaxed atmosphere mostly	

Job: Residential Assistant in college

+	−
Liked counseling the students a lot	Hated being the policeman
Enjoyed the independence	Not enough guidance about how to handle tough situations
I like it when I could help someone	

Job: Campus Newspaper – getting and writing up stories

+	−
Really enjoyed hearing people's stories	Stress of deadlines
Loved seeing my work in print—product was cool	Did not pay very much
When we finished the paper we were done and didn't take work home	Office politics about who got the good stories

Job: Law School

+	−
Some of the people were nice	Hated law school (although I did well)
Liked learning new legal concepts	Hated studying the law
	Hated competitive people in class
	Hated "Socratic Method"
	Didn't "get" the way to study until my third year

Job: Large Law Firm litigation associate

+	−
Liked the partner I worked with most closely	Didn't like the mission
Enjoyed learning new concepts	Hated the stress
Liked the money	Hated having to work when my disorganized partner gave me a job to do at the last minute
	Not enough mentoring
	Not sure what I was doing
	Lack of structure made me crazy
	Did not get to work with clients
	Felt isolated working behind closed doors doing research

This work history is an abbreviated profile of a made up client. What emerges from this profile are the following themes:

1. Enjoys *learning new things*
2. Enjoys *structured setting* with clear information about what to do
3. Likes to interact with people in a *team/collegial* setting
4. Wants to make enough *money* to feel secure
5. Likes personal interaction; needs to *interact with people* as part of the job
6. Like the *role of helping*, giving advice, teaching, guiding others
7. Needs to *avoid stress*
8. Needs *projects that end* so that work does not spill over to life outside of work
9. Likes to be *trusted* by the boss
10. Prefers a more *relaxed pace*
11. Needs to have a *mission* that s/he feels is worthwhile
12. Needs to *avoid isolation*

Once you identify the major themes, you have the elements that make up Essential Elements.

Create a list of the elements you need to have to be satisfied with your work, and create a list of elements you need to avoid to be satisfied with your work.

Using the example above, here is a list of essential elements for this person.

Essential Elements to Try to Get in His or Her Work Life

1. Uptick on the learning curve—learn new things on the job
2. Structure and clear definition of expectations
3. Team
4. Enough money to feel secure
5. Interactive role involving people as part of the job
6. The role of the helping person, teacher, guide, counselor
7. Projects that end, finality
8. Trusted to do the job
9. Mission that matters to me
10. Casual, relaxed pace
11. Mentoring

Here is a list of what this person should try to avoid.

Irritants to Avoid

1. High stress workplace
2. Fast pace
3. Isolation
4. Boredom
5. Lack of trust
6. Lack of structure
7. Lack of mentoring
8. Low pay
9. Projects that go on and on with no end in sight
10. Mission that does not matter*

Not all irritants must go on the above list. Many of them will simply be the opposite of an item on the list of essential elements. Try to put only the most irritating elements on this list, the ones you feel "allergic" to—for example, the "micromanager" boss, the "screamer" boss, the backbiting co-workers, or lack of control over your free time because of last-minute assignments. These are elements that drive some people crazy. Every person has his or her own unique list. The work history is a chance to think through these irritants to avoid those that are particularly annoying for you.

In some cases you may not have enough work experience to know what your hot buttons are, or, for that matter, to know what you absolutely have to have in your work life to be happy. The work history is a more useful vehicle for people who have had at least some work experience. The work history is also a work in progress. Some elements should be added or taken off the list as a work life evolves over the course of a career.

The themes that emerge in this exercise will usually continue to reappear throughout a person's work life. In some cases, however, the theme will become less salient over time. For example, a person who wants to

---

*Note that every person has a different idea about what matters and what does not matter. For one person, helping companies be successful is a perfectly good mission. For another person the mission has to be about helping poor people or indigent people, helping women and children, or trying to make the world a better place. This determination is idiosyncratic and personal.

have control over handling matters, interacting with clients, and being trusted to do the work will, in fact, grow into that role over time. If this associate keeps working hard, eventually s/he will become the partner who does have client contact and who is fully trusted to do the work. The work history is a snapshot of current work desires.

The next part of the exercise, however, is crucial because some people cannot continue to work hard in a currently upsetting workplace because they are too miserable. The next part of the exercise helps you to assess that level of dissatisfaction. If there is a severe mismatch between what someone needs in his or her work life and what s/he is getting, that person may need to conduct a job search for a better fitting job or career.

Now that you have a list of Essential Elements, you need to grade each one on a scale of 1 to 10 to reflect how much this element matters to you.

If you give an element a "10" (the highest need), then you should not take a job if you will have to do without this element in the workplace. As you rate each element, ask yourself thess questions:

"How much do I have to have this in my work life?"

"How much am I willing to 'give a little' on this?"

If you give an element something lower than a "5," it may not be important enough for you to keep on the list.

After you finish grading each Essential Element, then grade your list of Irritants to Avoid. When you are assessing your irritants, you are grading them on a scale of 1 to 10, with "10" reflecting your highest level of hate and irritation. As you go through your list of irritants, ask yourself these questions:

"How much do I hate this on a scale of 1 to 10?"

"How much am I willing to 'give a little' on this?"

See the samples of completed Essential Elements and Irritants to Avoid if Possible, on pages 159 and 160.

ESSENTIAL ELEMENTS FOR YOUR CAREER

Every person has a different set of essentials for a satisfying career or job. In the process of doing our career counseling work there have been recurrent themes. The summary of themes that we have identified appears below. Feel free to add this to the list of other ideas that occur to you.

SAMPLE

1. *LEARN NEW THINGS - uptick on learning curve*　　1 2 3 4 5 6 7 (8) 9 10

2. *STRUCTURE — I know what is expected of me*　　1 2 3 4 5 6 (7) 8 9 10

3. *TEAM/COLLEGIAL — Good, engaging, fun people who help each other*　　1 2 3 4 5 6 7 8 (9) 10

4. *ENOUGH MONEY — At least $90,000*　　1 2 3 4 5 6 (7) 8 9 10

5. *INTERACT WITH PEOPLE — Talk with clients directly*　　1 2 3 4 5 6 7 8 (9) 10

6. *ROLE OF HELPING PERSON — Teaching, advising, guiding*　　1 2 3 4 5 6 7 8 9 (10)

7. *PROJECTS THAT END — finality*　　1 2 3 4 5 6 7 (8) 9 10

8. *TRUSTED TO DO THE JOB — given responsibility, allowed to make decisions*　　1 2 3 4 5 6 (7) 8 9 10

9. *MISSION THAT MATTERS TO ME — Make the world a little better, not worse*　　1 2 3 4 5 6 7 8 9 (10)

10. *CASUAL, RELAXED PACE — Business casual is fine*　　1 2 3 4 5 6 7 (8) 9 10

11. *MENTORING — Allowed to ask questions, even stupid ones without feeling put down / Given guidance*　　1 2 3 4 5 6 7 (8) 9 10

IRRITANTS TO AVOID IF POSSIBLE

Some people tend to have allergies to aspects of the work world or to people in the workplace. Some people can deal with a micromanaging boss, for example, while others cannot stand to be micromanaged. Try to identify the irritants that are hard for you to deal with at your current and past places of work, or in your life generally.

SAMPLE

1. *HIGH STRESS WORKPLACE*   1 2 3 4 5 6 7 8 ⑨ 10

2. *FAST PACE*   1 2 3 4 5 6 7 8 ⑨ 10

3. *ISOLATION*   1 2 3 4 5 6 7 8 9 ⑩

4. *BOREDOM*   1 2 3 4 5 6 ⑦ 8 9 10

5. *LACK OF TRUST*   1 2 3 4 5 ⑥ 7 8 9 10

6. *LACK OF STRUCTURE*   1 2 3 4 5 ⑥ 7 8 9 10

7. *LACK OF MENTORING*   1 2 3 4 5 6 7 8 ⑨ 10

8. *LOW PAY*   1 2 3 4 5 6 ⑦ 8 9 10

9. *PROJECTS THAT ARE ENDLESS*   1 2 3 4 5 6 7 8 ⑨ 10

10. *MISSION THAT DOES NOT MATTER (TO ME)*   1 2 3 4 5 6 7 8 9 ⑩

11.   1 2 3 4 5 6 7 8 9 10

If you have followed these instructions, you now have a template for the type of job that would work well for you. We know no job is perfect, but if you can try to get many of these elements into your work life, you will be happier.

You can now use the template to vet your current job to see why you are not satisfied.

Use a different colored pen for this exercise. Go through each element and evaluate your current workplace. You are grading your workplace to see how it is doing in terms of <u>your needs</u>. For example, if you need to learn new things and you graded that an "8," and your job gives you that uptick on the learning curve you want, then put a colored dot about the "8" you circled. The job is meeting your needs on that score.

Look for serious mismatches between your template and the job you currently have. Any time there is a mismatch of 4 or more points, that should be considered serious.

For example, if you need the role of the helping person and you have given that a "10," and your current job gets a grade of "2" or "3," then you have a serious mismatch between what you need and what you are getting. This is one of the reasons you are not satisfied with your job.

What if you need a "Mission that Matters" and you give that a "10" but you grade your current job at a "1"? That is a mismatch of 9 points. Here is another serious mismatch of your aspirations and needs with a job that is not meeting those needs.

Whenever you have a serious mismatch of a deeply felt need with a job that is flunking your needs, you have the basis for career or job dissatisfaction. If you have even one of these mismatches, you are likely to be unhappy until and unless you can find work that is a better match.

If you have only slight mismatches between your template needs and the current job you are doing, you probably can hang in there and keep your current job to put bread on the table, while conducting a quest for a workplace or career direction that is an even better fit.

Next, grade your current workplace using the Irritants to Avoid template. Are you able to avoid high stress? You are looking for a "9"—how is your workplace doing on this score?

You really hate isolation. You give that a "10" on the hate scale. How much are you able to avoid isolation at your job?

Take a look at the examples on pages 163 and 164 and see how one person could fill out the form. In this sample template, the way the form is filled out shows a very high level of irritation and an inability to avoid the irritants that the person really hates.

This is a profile that shows a serious problem in terms of matching up the person's deeply felt needs to the reality of the job. This is a person who will need to look for a new job unless there is some other way to avoid the things s/he cannot stand.

You can also use your template to vet future job opportunities. When you have located an opportunity that you think could be good for you, go back to your template and think about whether this job is going to meet your needs.

If you gave the role of the helping person a "10," are you likely to get that?

If you gave feeling good about the mission a "10," will you feel that way about this job?

If you gave interacting with people a "9," will that be part of your work life?

How can you figure out if you will get what you need from a potential job? Your networking effort is the key to learning this information.

As you wind your way through the forest talking with the people who live there and have on-the-ground information about the workplace you are vetting, you can ask questions that help you to learn what you need to know.

"What is Chris like as a boss? Is he a micromanager? A screamer? Disorganized? Does he trust his associates to do the job?"

"What kind of work pace do people have over there? Do they bring work home at night and over the weekends?" If you talk with people in confidence, you can get information that is helpful to you to figure out if this work setting will be closer to your needs. One good way to learn this information is to find people who have recently left the workplace (within

ESSENTIAL ELEMENTS FOR YOUR CAREER

Every person has a different set of essentials for a satisfying career or job. In the process of doing our career counseling work there have been recurrent themes. The summary of themes that we have identified appears below. Feel free to add this to the list of other ideas that occur to you.

SAMPLE

1. *LEARN NEW THINGS - uptick on learning curve*
   1 2 3 4 5 6 7 (8) 9 10

2. *STRUCTURE — I know what is expected of me*
   1 2 3 4 5 6 (7) 8 9 10

3. *TEAM/COLLEGIAL — Good, engaging, fun people who help each other*
   1 2 3 4 5 6 7 8 (9) 10

4. *ENOUGH MONEY — At least $90,000*
   1 2 3 4 5 6 (7) 8 9 10

5. *INTERACT WITH PEOPLE — Talk with clients directly*
   1 2 3 4 5 6 7 8 (9) 10

6. *ROLE OF HELPING PERSON — Teaching, advising, guiding*
   1 2 3 4 5 6 7 8 9 (10)

7. *PROJECTS THAT END — finality*
   1 2 3 4 5 6 7 (8) 9 10

8. *TRUSTED TO DO THE JOB — given responsibility, allowed to make decisions*
   1 2 3 4 5 6 (7) 8 9 10

9. *MISSION THAT MATTERS TO ME — Make the world a little better, not worse*
   1 2 3 4 5 6 7 8 9 (10)

10. *CASUAL, RELAXED PACE — Business casual is fine*
    1 2 3 4 5 6 7 (8) 9 10

11. *MENTORING — Allowed to ask questions, even stupid ones without feeling put down / Given guidance*
    1 2 3 4 5 6 7 (8) 9 10

IRRITANTS TO AVOID IF POSSIBLE

Some people tend to have allergies to aspects of the work world or to people in the workplace. Some people can deal with a micromanaging boss, for example, while others cannot stand to be micromanaged. Try to identify the irritants that are hard for you to deal with at your current and past places of work, or in your life generally.

SAMPLE

1. *HIGH STRESS WORKPLACE*   1 2 3 4 5 6 7 8 (9) 10

2. *FAST PACE*   1 2 3 4 5 6 7 8 (9) 10

3. *ISOLATION*   1 2 3 4 5 6 7 8 9 (10)

4. *BOREDOM*   1 2 3 4 5 6 (7) 8 9 10

5. *LACK OF TRUST*   1 2 3 4 5 (6) 7 8 9 10

6. *LACK OF STRUCTURE*   1 2 3 4 5 (6) 7 8 9 10

7. *LACK OF MENTORING*   1 2 3 4 5 6 7 8 (9) 10

8. *LOW PAY*   1 2 3 4 5 6 (7) 8 9 10

9. *PROJECTS THAT ARE ENDLESS*   1 2 3 4 5 6 7 8 (9) 10

10. *MISSION THAT DOES NOT MATTER (TO ME)*   1 2 3 4 5 6 7 8 9 (10)

11.   1 2 3 4 5 6 7 8 9 10

the past year or two), and call them up and ask if they would be willing to talk with you. It sounds like this:

"I am considering taking a job at the firm you worked at two years ago. I was wondering if you would be willing to talk with me in absolute confidence about your experiences over there. I just want to be sure I will be able to obtain what I am looking for if I take this job."

How do you find people who have left that workplace? Most cities have an annual directory of lawyers which lists where they currently work. Try to find an old and new directory to figure out who is currently at the workplace. Next, you identify the people who left and use the current directory to locate their current workplaces. Then you call them up and ask for the chance to hear about their experiences.

Another source of this kind of information is anyone who is loosely affiliated with the workplace, such as spouses or friends of people who are or have been working at the workplace you are trying to vet.

Conclusion

The value of these exercises lies in the preparation and understanding you gain from doing the work that allows you to figure out the elements you need for a satisfying career. When you are networking for opportunities people will ask you what you want from your career. You need to know what you want. When you interview for a job, the interviewers with ask you what your long term plan is for your career. You need to be able to articulate that. If you are not happy with your career you need to under-stand why that is and have an idea about what would make you happier.

Even though no job is perfect, some are better than others. When we know ourselves well enough to know what we are looking for, and under-stand the work settings that will bring out the best in us, we will have more productive and effective job searches.

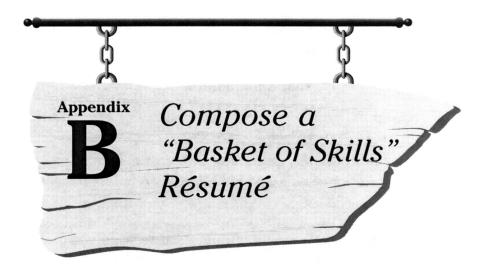

Appendix B

Compose a "Basket of Skills" Résumé

Many job seekers prepare a chronological résumé. There is nothing wrong with that. That type of résumé highlights longevity at one work-place, a consistent job history, and loyalty.

In a networking search, however, the job seeker is networking in person with many people. The idea of an in-person networking search is to show up for a breakfast, lunch, dinner, or coffee, or by invitation at the contact person's office, and have a conversation that opens doors.

There is a lot of information that a job seeker is trying to talk about with the contact person. In fact, it may be difficult to cover all topics that a networker wants to try to cover in the time frame of a lunch or a cup of coffee.

For that reason it is important to prepare a résumé for networking purposes that makes it very easy for the contact person to grasp the networker's background immediately. The "skills-based" style résumé does a good job of that.

As illustrated on the following pages, a skill-based résumé or "basket of skills" style résumé has a skills summary at the top of the résumé. That summary can be altered depending on the contact person the networker is meeting with. The skills summary should highlight the core competencies that match up with the contact person's likely con-nections for the networker.

Your name
Your home address
Your phone number
Your e-mail address

SKILLS SUMMARY

[Start with your practice area, then follow with your area(s) of expertise. This shows what you can do for the employer without further training.]

Illustration

Income partner with eight years of litigation and regulatory experience. Responsibilities include counseling, drafting motions and briefs, taking over 30 depositions, preparing pretrial memoranda, participating as lead attorney in over 40 regulatory hearings, legal research and writing, analyzing and drafting legislation, managing large document reviews including associate oversight in complex litigation matters.

EXPERIENCE

[Next, tell the reader in brief form where you have worked, when you were there, and your role at that job.]

Illustration

Firm A LLP, Chicago, Illinois
Associate, Commercial Litigation, 2000–Present; Summer Associate, 1999

Firm B LLP, Chicago, Illinois
Summer Associate, 1998

EDUCATION

[Next, tell the reader your education, including honors you earned.]

Illustration

University of Illinois College of Law. J.D. *with distinction* 1996
  Law Review Notes Editor, Research Assistant for Prof. —— on regulatory issues and sustainable energy, co-author of "——".

Bradley University B.S. Psychology, *cum laude*, 1993

[Next, list professional publications, memberships, community involvement, and interests, especially if the interests are ones that might open the door to a conversation with your contact person, such as a shared interest or unusual pursuit. Try to keep all of this on one page.]

[You can also have a second page of Professional Accomplishments that briefly describe in bulleted form your significant achievements. These can be talking points for your meeting.]

C Master List of People and Places

The focus of your networking meetings should be on learning what is happening in the neighborhood(s) you think you want to join, what is going on in the villages behind the castles you want to be a part of.

To that end, your conversations with knights and wizards should focus at least in part on the places you are finding out about that could be good matches for you, and the other people in the neighborhood doing the work you think you want to do.

The Master List of People and Places should grow as you learn more about your targeted neighborhoods.

One way to create a Master List is to simply identify every person you want to try to meet up with and on another page list every workplace you would like to learn more about. You simply keep growing these lists as your knowledge grows. Every time you go to a networking meeting you print off the list and bring it to the meeting.

At the meeting, pull out your lists and do the following:

> ➤ Ask your contact person to review each list and check off people he knows and would permit you to contact to learn more about the market in general and specific workplaces.
> ➤ Better yet, ask if he would be willing to send an e-mail on your behalf to someone over there who is "nice," to help you make that next connection.
> ➤ You also want to ask your contact person to review the list of places that your think could be a good match for you.

➤ Then ask him what, if anything, he has heard about the places where he knows people and whether he has heard if any of these places are busy, active, and growing, and have a good reputation, meaning people like to work there.

Another way to create a useful Master List of people and places is to use the format on the following page. In these Master Lists the networker has figured out the castles of interest, and is filling in the key keepers, the knights, and the wizards and is keeping notes about his or her progress. See Exhibit One.

Exhibit One: Master List of People and Places

Castles	Key Keepers	Knights/ Wizards	Notes

Index

Virtual Law Practice: How to Deliver Legal Services Online
By Stephanie L. Kimbro

The legal market has recently experienced a dramatic shift as lawyers seek out alternative methods of practicing law and providing more affordable legal services. Virtual law practice is revolutionizing the way the public receives legal services and how legal professionals work with clients. If you are interested in this form of practicing law, *Virtual Law Practice* will help you:

- Responsibly deliver legal services online to your clients
- Successfully set up and operate a virtual law office
- Establish a virtual law practice online through a secure, client-specific portal
- Manage and market your virtual law practice
- Understand state ethics and advisory opinions
- Find more flexibility and work/life balance in the legal profession

The Lawyer's Guide to Microsoft Word 2007
By Ben M. Schorr

Microsoft Word is one of the most used applications in the Microsoft Office suite—there are few applications more fundamental than putting words on paper. Most lawyers use Word and few of them get everything they can from it. Because the documents you create are complex and important—your law practice depends, to some degree, upon the quality of the documents you produce and the efficiency with which you can produce them. Focusing on the tools and features that are essential for lawyers in their everyday practice, *The Lawyer's Guide to Microsoft Word* explains in detail the key components to help make you more effective, more efficient and more successful.

iPad in One Hour for Lawyers
By Tom Mighell

Whether you are a new or a more advanced iPad user, *iPad in One Hour for Lawyers* takes a great deal of the mystery and confusion out of using your iPad. Ideal for lawyers who want to get up to speed swiftly, this book presents the essentials so you don't get bogged down in technical jargon and extraneous features and apps. In just six, short lessons, you'll learn how to:

- Quickly Navigate and Use the iPad User Interface
- Set Up Mail, Calendar, and Contacts
- Create and Use Folders to Multitask and Manage Apps
- Add Files to Your iPad, and Sync Them
- View and Manage Pleadings, Case Law, Contracts, and other Legal Documents
- Use Your iPad to Take Notes and Create Documents
- Use Legal-Specific Apps at Trial or in Doing Research

Find Info Like a Pro, Volume 1: Mining the Internet's Publicly Available Resources for Investigative Research
By Carole A. Levitt and Mark E. Rosch

This complete hands-on guide shares the secrets, shortcuts, and realities of conducting investigative and background research using the sources of publicly available information available on the Internet. Written for legal professionals, this comprehensive desk book lists, categorizes, and describes hundreds of free and fee-based Internet sites. The resources and techniques in this book are useful for investigations; depositions; locating missing witnesses, clients, or heirs; and trial preparation, among other research challenges facing legal professionals. In addition, a CD-ROM is included, which features clickable links to all of the sites contained in the book.

How to Start and Build a Law Practice, Platinum Fifth Edition
By Jay G. Foonberg

This classic ABA bestseller has been used by tens of thousands of lawyers as the comprehensive guide to planning, launching, and growing a successful practice. It's packed with over 600 pages of guidance on identifying the right location, finding clients, setting fees, managing your office, maintaining an ethical and responsible practice, maximizing available resources, upholding your standards, and much more. You'll find the information you need to successfully launch your practice, run it at maximum efficiency, and avoid potential pitfalls along the way. If you're committed to starting—and growing—your own practice, this one book will give you the expert advice you need to make it succeed for years to come.

Social Media for Lawyers: The Next Frontier
By Carolyn Elefant and Nicole Black

The world of legal marketing has changed with the rise of social media sites such as Linkedin, Twitter, and Facebook. Law firms are seeking their companies attention with tweets, videos, blog posts, pictures, and online content. Social media is fast and delivers news at record pace. This book provides you with a practical, goal-centric approach to using social media in your law practice that will enable you to identify social media platforms and tools that fit your practice and implement them easily, efficiently, and ethically.

30-Day Risk-Free Order Form
Call Today! 1-800-285-2221
Monday–Friday, 7:30 AM – 5:30 PM, Central Time

Qty	Title	LPM Price	Regular Price	Total
_____	The Lawyer's Guide to Collaboration Tools and Technologies: Smart Ways to Work Together (5110589)	$59.95	$ 89.95	$_____
_____	Google for Lawyers: Essential Search Tips and Productivity Tools (5110704)	47.95	79.95	$_____
_____	The Lawyer's Guide to Adobe Acrobat, Third Edition (5110588)	49.95	79.95	$_____
_____	The Electronic Evidence and Discovery Handbook: Forms, Checklists, and Guidelines (5110569)	99.95	129.95	$_____
_____	The 2011 Solo and Small Firm Legal Technology Guide (5110716)	54.95	89.95	$_____
_____	The Lawyer's Guide to LexisNexis CaseMap (5110715)	47.95	79.95	$_____
_____	Virtual Law Practice: How to Deliver Legal Services Online (5110707)	47.95	79.95	$_____
_____	The Lawyer's Guide to Microsoft Word 2007 (5110697)	49.95	69.95	$_____
_____	iPadin One Hour for Lawyers (5110719)	19.95	34.95	$_____
_____	Find Info Like a Pro, V1: Mining the . . . (5110708)	47.95	79.95	$_____
_____	How to Start and Build a Law Practice, Platinum Fifth Edition (5110508)	57.95	69.95	$_____
_____	Social Media for Lawyers: The Next Frontier (5110710)	47.95	79.95	$_____

*Postage and Handling	
$10.00 to $49.99	$5.95
$50.00 to $99.99	$7.95
$100.00 to $199.99	$9.95
$200.00+	$12.95

**Tax
DC residents add 6%
IL residents add 9.75%

*Postage and Handling $_____
**Tax $_____
TOTAL $_____

PAYMENT

❑ Check enclosed (to the ABA)

❑ Visa ❑ MasterCard ❑ American Express

_____
Account Number   Exp. Date   Signature

Name _____ Firm _____

Address _____

City _____ State _____ Zip _____

Phone Number _____ E-Mail Address _____

Guarantee
If—for any reason—you are not satisfied with your purchase, you may return it within 30 days of receipt for a complete refund of the price of the book(s). No questions asked!

Mail: ABA Publication Orders, P.O. Box 10892, Chicago, Illinois 60610-0892
♦ **Phone: 1-800-285-2221** ♦ **FAX: 312-988-5568**

E-Mail: abasvcctr@americanbar.org ♦ **Internet: http://www.lawpractice.org/catalog**

Are You in Your Element?

Tap into the Resources of the ABA Law Practice Management Section

ABA Law Practice Management Section Membership Benefits

The ABA Law Practice Management Section (LPM) is a professional membership organization of the American Bar Association that helps lawyers and other legal professionals with the business of practicing law. LPM focuses on providing information and resources in the core areas of marketing, management, technology, and finance through its award-winning magazine, teleconference series, Webzine, educational programs (CLE), Web site, and publishing division. For more than thirty years, LPM has established itself as a leader within the ABA and the profession-at-large by producing the world's largest legal technology conference (ABA TECHSHOW®) each year. In addition, LPM's publishing program is one of the largest in the ABA, with more than eighty-five titles in print.

In addition to significant book discounts, LPM Section membership offers these benefits:

ABA TECHSHOW

Membership includes a $100 discount to ABA TECHSHOW, the world's largest legal technology conference & expo!

Teleconference Series

Convenient, monthly CLE teleconferences on hot topics in marketing, management, technology and finance. Access educational opportunities from the comfort of your office chair – today's practical way to earn CLE credits!

LAW|PRACTICE
THE BUSINESS OF PRACTICING LAW

Law Practice Magazine

Eight issues of our award-winning *Law Practice* magazine, full of insightful articles and practical tips on Marketing/Client Development, Practice Management, Legal Technology, and Finance.

Law Practice TODAY

Law Practice Today

LPM's unique Web-based magazine covers all the hot topics in law practice management today — identify current issues, face today's challenges, find solutions quickly. Visit www.lawpracticetoday.org.

LAW TECHNOLOGY TODAY

Law Technology Today

LPM's newest Webzine focuses on legal technology issues in law practice management — covering a broad spectrum of the technology, tools, strategies and their implementation to help lawyers build a successful practice. Visit www.lawtechnologytoday.org.

LawPractice.news
Monthly news and information from the ABA Law Practice Management Section

LawPractice.news

Brings Section news, educational opportunities, book releases, and special offers to members via e-mail each month.

To learn more about the ABA Law Practice Management Section, visit www.lawpractice.org or call 1-800-285-2221.

MARKETING • MANAGEMENT • TECHNOLOGY • FINANCE

HELLO
my name is

Value

Join the ABA Law Practice Management Section Today!

Value is . . .

Resources that help you become a better lawyer:
- Up to 40% off LPM publications
- Six Issues of *Law Practice* magazine, both print and electronic versions
- Twelve issues of our monthly Webzine, *Law Practice Today*
- Your connection to Section news and events through *LawPractice.news*
- Discounted registration on "Third Thursday" CLE Teleconference Series and LPM conferences

Networking with industry experts while improving your skills at:
- ABA TECHSHOW
- ABA Law Firm Marketing Strategies Conference
- ABA Women Rainmakers Mid-Career Workshop
- LPM Quarterly Meetings

Opportunity given exclusively to our members:
- Writing for LPM periodicals and publications
- Joining ABA Women Rainmakers
- Becoming a better leader through committee involvement
- Listing your expertise in the LPM Speakerbase

**Members of LPM get up to 40% off publications like this one.
Join today and start saving!**

www.lawpractice.org • 1.800.285.2221

ABA LAWPRACTICEMANAGEMENTSECTION

MARKETING • MANAGEMENT • TECHNOLOGY • FINANCE